FINANCIAL PLANNING WITH EMPLOYEE BENEFITS

Mel Albin, Ph.D., M.B.A.
Noel A. Johnson
Andrew Jacobs
Howard M. Sachs, J.D.

CRISP PUBLICATIONS, INC.
Los Altos, California

FINANCIAL PLANNING WITH EMPLOYEE BENEFITS

Mel Albin, Ph.D., M.B.A.
Noel A. Johnson
Andrew Jacobs
Howard M. Sachs, J.D.

CREDITS
Editor: **Michael G. Crisp and Tony Hicks**
Designer: **Carol Harris**
Typesetting: **Interface Studio**
Cover Design: **Carol Harris**
Artwork: **Ralph Mapson**

Crisp books are distributed in Canada by Reid Publishing, Ltd., P.O. Box 7267, Oakville, Ontario, Canada L6J 6L6.

In Australia by Career Builders, P.O. Box 1051, Springwood, Brisbane, Queensland, Australia 4127.

And in New Zealand by Career Builders, P.O. Box 571, Manurewa, New Zealand.

Library of Congress Catalog Card Number 89-61793
Albin, Mel; Johnson, Noel; Jacobs, Andrew, and Sachs, Howard
Financial Planning with Employee Benefits
ISBN 0-931961-90-4

DEDICATION

Bob James, the founder of Raymond James & Associates, Inc., had a vision of the need to plan first by assembling data, building a team of professional advisors, and only then buy investments after careful shopping. Tom James, his son and current Chairman of the Board of RJ Financial, has supported the concept of financial planning through thick and thin, making his father's vision a reality.

We dedicate this book to them with admiration and thanks.

Mel Albin

Noel A. Johnson

Andrew Jacobs

Howard M. Sachs

ACKNOWLEDGMENTS

We want to thank those who have supported our work over the years, particularly Terry Smith, Bob Shuck, Harvey Hertz, Dick Weinberger, Larry Silver, Ann Clark, Debbie Czodli, Steve Faber, Cindy Kelty and countless others. Particularly, we want to thank Tami Pedatella, our Financial Planning Assistant, who has labored hard to make us socially acceptable. Mel and Noel want to thank their wives Karen and Ollie respectively for their help and support for their endeavors.

TO THE READER

Employees of major corporations have a complex package of benefits provided to them by their employers. Employees may not understand how to use these benefits when preparing their personal financial plan. The purpose of this book is to educate employees to use their benefits to help achieve financial independence.

The strategies offered are only suggestions. Implementation should not be attempted without first consulting your financial advisors and benefits personnel.

CONTENTS

CONTENTS (Continued)

CONTENTS (Continued)

PART I

Introduction to Financial Planning

WHAT IS FINANCIAL PLANNING?

"Personal financial planning is nothing more than the development and implementation of a comprehensive plan to help a person achieve his or her specific financial goals." Alan Klosowski, CFP, *Personal Financial Fitness*, Crisp Publications, Los Altos, California.

To build a basic financial plan, you need to consider:

- PROTECTION OF INCOME
  —Health Insurance
  —Disability Insurance
- SECURITY FOR SURVIVORS
  —Life Insurance
- A RETIREMENT PROGRAM
  —Pension
  —Investments
- TAX-REDUCTION STRATEGIES
  —Tax-Deferred Savings Plan
- A SYSTEM OF RECORD KEEPING

This probably looks like the package of benefits provided by your employer. In essence, your employer has begun the financial planning process for you!

An independent businessperson must hire professionals to keep records, prepare annual statements, withhold taxes, and administer the benefit package. Fortunately, your employer already does this for you as part of your compensation.

Your benefits package is a significant part of your total compensation. But it is up to you to make the best use of it.

THE BENEFITS OF FINANCIAL PLANNING

Financial planning seeks to increase all forms of income and reduce all forms of expenses while helping you build and maintain a satisfying lifestyle. It does not start with buying investments. It begins with setting goals and developing strategies. Financial planning should be done with advisors, but the final decision should always remain with the individual who is earning the money to be managed.

Personal financial security in America today comes from three main sources:

- **The individual's effort** by means of work, savings, investing, and personal insurance.
- **The employer's contribution** through employee benefits such as health insurance, pensions, savings plans, and life insurance.
- **The government's contribution** including Social Security benefits and services, and legislation to protect and define employee benefits.

Financial planning helps you coordinate these three sources to achieve and maintain financial security. It does this by applying principles of business management to the management of personal finances. All aspects of personal money management are analyzed, including:

- Career management
- Employee benefits
- Banking
- Budgeting
- Consumer purchases
- Insurance planning and risk management
- Investment planning
- Tax planning
- Retirement planning
- Estate planning

ACHIEVING FINANCIAL OBJECTIVES WITH EMPLOYEE BENEFITS

In many ways, your package of employee benefits will help you achieve your financial objectives. Employment shapes your lifestyle and enables you to achieve these essential personal and financial goals:

- An income sufficient to build and maintain a lifestyle.
- Wealth to buy houses, cars, and consumer products and services.
- Investments for future goals:
  —providing for children's education.
  —starting a business.
  —a financially secure retirement.
- Protection of income for yourselves and your survivors.
- Health care for you and your family members.
- Maintaining a savings reserve for emergencies and special events.

Employee benefits are easy to use because they are often either funded from your regular pay or operate automatically, with little or no cost or effort to you.

RECOMMENDATION

Use your employee benefits to maximum advantage before you purchase or use other financial services to build your financial goals.

HOW TO BEGIN

First—List some of your major financial goals:

____

____

____

Second—List some of your most pressing financial concerns now:

____

____

____

Third—Begin financial planning by organizing information. Here is a list of documents you need. Check off each document as you collect it.

- ☐ 1. Your tax returns for the past two years
- 2. Information about your investments
  - ☐ a. Tax Shelters
  - ☐ b. IRAs, TSAs, Keogh
  - ☐ c. Income Properties (Mortgage Amount)
  - ☐ d. CDs, Money Market
  - ☐ e. Brokerage Account and Mutual Fund Statements
  - ☐ f. Credit Union and Bank Accounts
  - ☐ g. Trust Accounts
- ☐ 3. A recent statement of company's employee benefits
- 4. Company Manual Explaining Benefits Provided
  - ☐ a. Group Insurance
  - ☐ b. Disability Coverage
  - ☐ c. Pension/Profit Sharing
  - ☐ d. 401K Contributions
- ☐ 5. Recent Company Payroll Check Stub
- ☐ 6. Family Budget
- ☐ 7. Personal Insurance Policies/Business Policies
- ☐ 8. Copy of Current Wills and/or Trusts
- ☐ 9. Balance of Mortgages (Approximate)
- ☐ 10. Balance of Outstanding Debts

HIRING ADVISORS

Once information is organized, you may find that you need to investigate building a team of professionals. This team could include:

- Employee Benefits Officers
- Financial Planners
- Tax Advisors
- Attorneys
- Real Estate Agents
- Insurance Advisors
- Investment Representatives
- Bankers

But before you hire professional advisors, ask yourself if you really need their help. Is your financial situation complex enough to warrant the expense?

To locate competent advisors, obtain referrals from:

—other professionals

—friends or family members

—professional organizations and licensing agencies

Like any other consumer product or service, shop for the best value. If you are not satisfied with an advisor, look for someone else who meets your needs.

QUESTIONS TO ASK

Begin the selection process by asking the following questions of all advisors:

- How much do you charge for services?
- How and when am I billed for your services?
- What credentials and education and experience do you have?
- How long have you been in business?
- Is there a charge for a preliminary consultation?
- Will you put our agreement in writing?
- What percentage of your practice is devoted to cases like mine?

If you are not satisfied with any of these answers, go to the next person on your list.

TYPES OF ADVISORS

- **WHAT THEY DO**
- **WHEN YOU NEED THEM**
- **WHAT TO ASK THEM**

Employee Benefits Officers

What They Do:

There are a variety of employment settings in which you find benefits advisors:

- Small employers who may have only one personnel advisor.
- Large employers who may have many levels of benefits officers in both the home and regional offices, including specialists trained in advising employees on their benefits.

Find out who, in your organization can advise you about your benefits. Large organizations often have a benefits office you many call or visit. It is your responsibility to obtain advice and information regarding your benefits.

When You Need Them:

You need to talk to a benefits advisor when:

- You join an organization.
- You plan to retire or leave an organization.
- You are promoted or change jobs.
- A tax law change affects your benefits.
- You get married, divorced, or have children.
- You or a family member have a health problem.
- You need information to prepare a financial plan.

What To Ask Them:

- What summaries and booklets can you provide on my benefits?
- How often are my benefits statements updated?
- Who should I contact for specific benefits questions?
- Do you provide educational programs on my benefits?
- How would my beneficiaries contact you in the event of my disability or death?

Financial Planners

What They Do:

A financial planner can assist you in:
- Organizing your financial data.
- Identifying financial goals.
- Developing a financial plan and coordinating your finances.
- Selecting strategies for implementing solutions.
- Implementing your plan and monitoring your progress.

When You Need Them:

You need a financial planner when:
- You have financial problems that need solutions.
- You retire.
- You receive an inheritance.
- You change jobs.
- You start a business or sell one.
- You marry or divorce.
- You do anything that significantly changes your use of income or assets.

What To Ask:

- Are you registered with the SEC, NASD, New York Stock Exchange or State Securities Agency?
- How will you prepare my financial plan?
- How many investment companies and financial services do you represent?
- Whom will I work with on a regular basis?
- How do you stay abreast of the latest financial developments?
- How will you be involved in implementing the plan you suggest?
- Will the plan be in writing?
- How often is the plan reviewed?
- How will you be compensated?
- Will you give me a written agreement explaining what you will do for me?

There are three types of compensation arrangements:
- Fee only financial plan
- Commissions only financial plan
- Fee and/or commission financial plan

A written estimate detailing services to be provided and fees to be charged must be obtained.

Tax Advisors

What They Do:

There are three types of tax advisors:

- High volume walk-in tax preparation services.
- CPAs or enrolled agents who have passed a written exam.
- Tax attorneys for handling complex legal tax issues.

When You Need Them:

Common concerns that may lead you to consult a tax advisor are:

- A need to reduce your taxes.
- Complex tax regulations and filing procedures.
- A special tax problem you cannot answer without help.
- The receipt of a large sum of money from retirement, inheritance, an investment, a legal settlement, or the sale/purchase of a home, business or other asset.

What To Ask:

- Do you provide tax planning services?
- Are you available for advice all year or only at tax time?
- What are your fees for preparing taxes and giving tax advice?
- Will you accompany me to the IRS in the event of an audit? Does this cost extra?
- Will I get a tax refund?
- Am I over-withholding or under-withholding taxes?

Attorneys

What They Do:

Attorneys are trained to help you use the legal system to solve legal problems. There are many types of attorneys, specializing in different aspects of legal services. They can advise you, represent you in court, and write legal documents and contracts.

When You Need Them:

Before hiring an attorney, ask yourself:

Can I handle this problem myself?
Is this a complex matter that is likely to go to court?
Will complex legal filings follow?
Is a large amount of money, property, or time involved?

Seek Legal Advice When You:

Experience property damage or personal injury.
Need a will or trust.
Are considering bankruptcy.
Are starting a new business.
Want to divorce, marry or adopt a child.
Want to understand a contract.
Want to understand and solve estate issues and problems.
Have a legal or criminal problem.
Are closing on the purchase of real estate.

What To Ask:

- Is there any charge for a preliminary consultation?
- What percentage of your practice is devoted to cases like mine?
- Who will work on my case—you, an assistant, or a paralegal assistant?
- If we have a dispute, will you submit to binding arbitration?
- How long will it take to complete my case, and what will the approximate costs be?
- How will you keep me informed on a regular basis?
- Do you require a retainer?
- Do you work for a flat fee?
- Do you accept contingency fee arrangements?

Real Estate Agents

What They Do:

There are many kinds of real estate advisors. Most sell real estate and earn commissions. Some real estate advisors charge fees for their services. Realtors may have extensive training and experience in dealing with various real estate issues.

When You Need Them:

Use a real estate agent to:

- Qualify buyers or prepare you to qualify as a real estate buyer.
- Protect your privacy during the sale of real estate.
- Get the best price for you as a buyer or a seller.
- Give you access to a wide range of buyers.
- Help you relocate to another city.

What To Ask:

Sellers ask:

- Will you appraise my property for no fee?
- What sales price would you recommend for my property?
- How do you plan to market my property?
- How much will you charge me?
- What kind of listing contract is required (exclusive right to sell or exclusive agency contract)?
- How experienced are you in selling my type of property?
- How familiar are you with homes in my immediate area?

Buyers ask:

- Whom do you legally represent, the property buyer, seller, or both?
- Will you agree to represent me exclusively?

Insurance Agents

What They Do:

There are two broad lines of insurance:

- Life, health, and disability.
- Property, auto, casualty, and business.

The two basic kinds of agents are:

- Independent agents who represent a wide variety of companies.
- Company agents who represent the services of one company.

When You Need Them:

You need insurance advice when you:

- Buy a new home, car, or boat.
- Start a business or partnership.
- Get married or divorced.
- Start a family.
- Plan to retire.
- Face a death in your family.

What To Ask:

- Are you an independent agent, or do you represent one company?
- Do you specialize in some lines of insurance, or are you a general agent?
- How long have you been in business in this area?
- Are you compensated with commissions, fees, or both?

Investment Representatives

What They Do:

Investment representatives are available in many different institutions such as banks, small independent firms, specialty firms, financial planning firms, full service and discount brokerage firms. All offer different skills, licenses, advisement capabilities and services. There are two major categories of investment representatives:

1. Stockbrokers—Stockbrokers have a general securities license to sell stocks, bonds, mutual funds, and limited partnerships. They may also be licensed to sell commodities, insurance, or annuities.
   - Full service brokers provide research and investment advice and normally a full range of investments and services.
   - Discount brokers are commonly associated with banks and discount brokerage firms. Generally, they provide no research or investment advice and process transactions based only on your initiative.
   - Institutional brokers specialize in trading for large organizations, pension plans, and other high volume clients.
   - Specialty firms such as penny stock firms offer securities that are not normally traded on major stock exchanges.
2. National Association of Security Dealers (NASD) representatives—NASD representatives sell only managed investments such as mutual funds.They are not licensed to sell stocks and bonds. They may be licensed to sell limited partnerships and variable insurance contracts.

When You Need Them:

Use a stockbroker when you:

- Have existing securities that need analysis.
- Own securities that you want to use as collateral for a loan.
- Want research on future investments.
- Have sufficient cash on hand to warrant the purchase of individual shares of stock, bonds, mutual funds, limited partnerships, etc.
- Enjoy trading securities and want to have a close relationship with a brokerage firm to assist you in executing your trades.
- Are an aggressive investor and want to trade penny stocks, options, or commodities.
- Want to trade stocks, bonds, or other investments in your self-directed IRA or pension plan.

Investment Representatives (Continued)

When You Need Them:

Use a discount broker when you want:

- Low transaction costs.
- To do your own trading without advice.
- To do your own research.

Use a NASD representative when you want:

- Advice on selecting managed accounts such as mutual funds, limited partnerships and variable insurance contracts.
- To start an investment accumulation program for major future goals like your child's college education or your own retirement.

What To Ask:

Some questions you should ask your investment representative:

- How long have you been in business as an investment representative?
- What kinds of services does your firm offer?
- What kinds of special experiences have you had in advising clients like me?
- Who will be handling my account besides you?
- What statements of my account will you provide, and how often?

Bankers

What They Do:

There are many kinds of bankers ranging from tellers to highly trained and experienced personal banking or trust officers. Bankers can help you invest cash, provide you with trust offices for a large estate, leverage real estate, buy and sell stock, and establish loans.

The differences between commercial banks, savings banks and credit are rapidly disappearing as government regulations change.

When You Need Them:

Use bankers to:

- Protect cash in interest bearing, insured accounts.
- Provide a trustee for your trust if either:
  —Your state of domicile prohibits you from being your own trustee in a living trust.
  —You prefer professional trusteeship to your own or another family member's administration.
- Free up home equity through low cost refinancing of your primary residence.
- Finance real estate or business purchases.

What To Ask:

- What services can you provide me?
- Do you have the authority to make the decision I want?
- Who will assist me in receiving the banking services I need or when I have a problem?

FREE FINANCIAL INFORMATION

Seminars

Perhaps the best way to obtain free information on financial matters is to attend public seminars offered by investment firms, accounting firms, law firms, banks, and real estate companies. When conducted by a responsible firm, these seminars can be quite informative.

Reading

There are some very useful books, magazines and brochures to read when doing financial planning.

- Start by reading over your benefits statements and manuals to familiarize yourself with what you already have.
- Read financial planning texts such as:
  Personal Financial Fitness 2/e, Klosowski, Crisp Publications, or
  Money Dynamics for the 1990's, by Venita VanCaspel
- Read major magazines like *Money, Time,* or *Newsweek* that print articles on financial planning.
- Your local newspaper may also contain special articles on the latest information on changes in tax laws, market conditions, etc.

Now you've begun thinking about goal setting, using your employee benefits as a basis for financial planning, and selecting advisors to help build financial security, the next chapter will focus on financial concerns that arise in different stages of life. This information will help you to better understand your financial goals and needs at various stages of the life cycle.

PART II

Life-Cycle Financial Planning

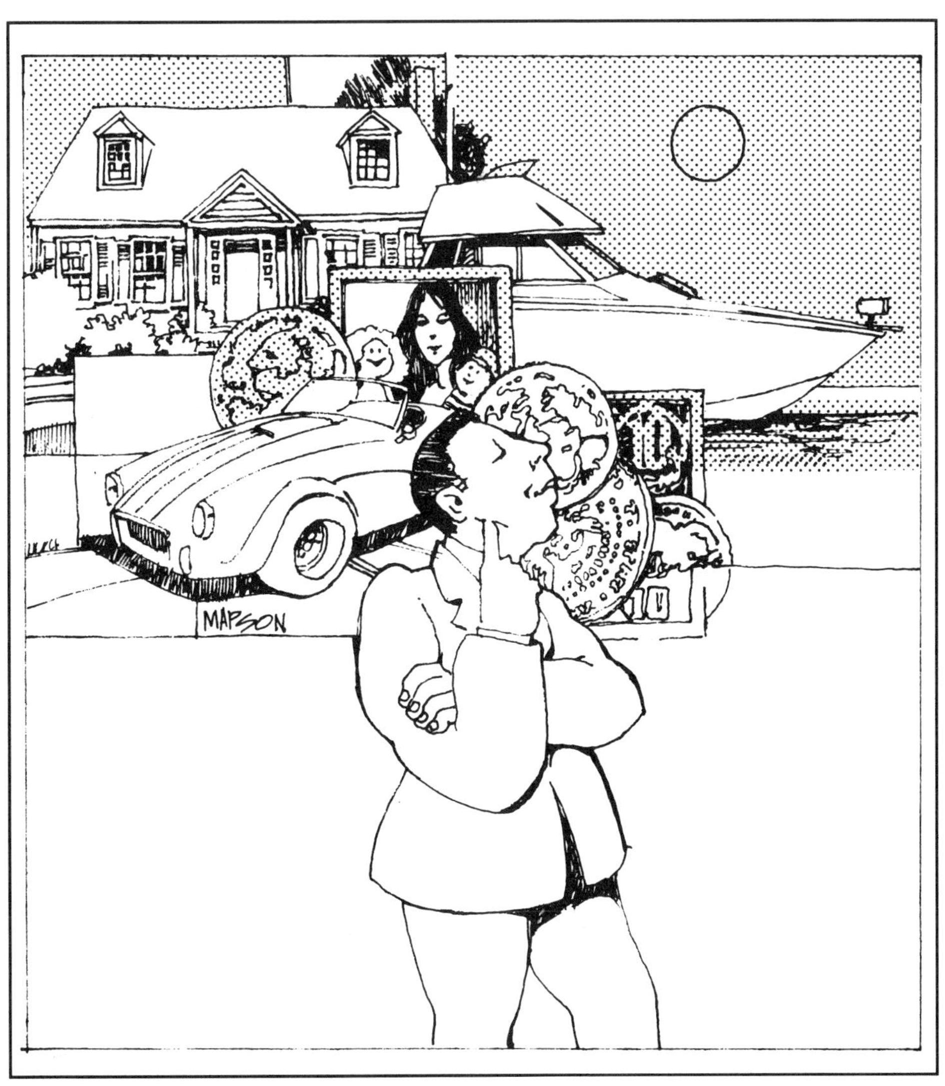

BENEFITS FOR YOUR LIFETIME

Life used to be simple. People would work hard, retire and soon expire. Lengthy retirement is a modern phenomenon. In the past, few workers lived many years beyond their retirement and even fewer had sufficient assets for a comfortable retirement.

Since F.D. Roosevelt's administration during the Great Depression, we have witnessed the creation of Social Security, pension plans, employee savings plans and stock option plans, employer-sponsored life and disability insurance, as well as health care plans with even wider coverage. These benefits now cover tens of millions of employees.

Today's complex benefits packages can pose dilemmas for employees, including:

- Mobility within the work force often leaves employees without the full vesting necessary for financial independence. Recent changes in the tax laws have shortened vesting schedules on retirement plans, and savings plans are now more portable than ever before.
- New tax incentives encourage employers to broaden the benefits they offer employees. The increasingly complex portfolios of employee benefits require more careful financial planning and record keeping.
- Planning for retirement which should start early in an employee's career. Today's employees need more time to accumulate assets because they will live longer, more active lives in retirement.

Financial plans can help solve the dilemmas that result from changes in the employee life cycle. Financial planning is essential for every employee but is never the same for individual employees. This is why it is important to carefully read this book and apply your specific situation to the information that is presented.

SINGLE EMPLOYEES

Single employees without children need to consider income continuation through disability insurance supplements. They also need to consider maximum funding of savings programs. Since they rely solely on their own income, financial independence before and after retirement should be a primary focus.

Young singles need liquidity for short-term goals, such as home purchase, car purchase, or getting married. Payroll deducted savings plans, credit unions, and after-tax savings plan contributions are best for this purpose.

Single employees may want to consider sheltering their benefits packages from financial disruption due to future marriages—and, perhaps, divorces. An attorney can advise you about the use of prenuptial agreements to protect what may be substantial vested employee benefits.

SINGLES NEED TO PLAN AHEAD, TOO!

EMPLOYEES WHO ARE PARENTS

Parents who want to save money for their children's college expenses should consider after-tax savings plan contributions to minimize penalties and taxes upon early withdrawals for college.* Some profit-sharing plans or 401K programs allow parents who make pretax contributions to borrow money from their plans to fund college tuition.

Ask the benefits administrator at your company about how best to use company benefits for college education costs. Savings for short term goals may be done through credit unions or other tax-controlled savings programs outside of the company. Parents can often buy U.S. Savings Bonds through payroll deduction. These E-Bonds mature in 5–10 years. Tax is due when the bonds are cashed. There is no tax if used for qualified education expenses. They can also build up cash values in personal or company cash-value life insurance policies. Cash values can often be borrowed for college expenses with no income taxes and little or no cost.

Parents should ensure that all family members are sufficiently covered by company health insurance plans. This often costs extra but is usually less expensive than purchasing coverage outside the company. It is wise to compare company supplemental insurance costs with outside programs.

A career change or job relocation can disrupt pay, benefits, lifestyle, and educational plans. Be sure the change produces income, benefits, and lifestyle features that justify any move. Changing companies often prohibits participation in deferred savings plans for up to one year. If job changes occur too frequently, vesting schedules may be impaired. This will result in substantial forfeitures of accumulated non-vested benefits.

Single working parents make up a sizeable segment of the work force. This group often faces difficulty providing for the financial well-being of their families. It is important for single parents to maintain secure employment with employers who provide a wide range of benefits. It is also wise for single parents to secure supplemental disability and/or life insurance if they are not fully protected at work.

---

* The IRS has stringent requirements regarding the use of these assets for college education costs. You must first deplete all other liquid assets and apply for a hardship ruling before you can use these funds without tax penalties.

AGE 25–45: ''BABY BOOMER'' FINANCIAL DILEMMAS

An interesting paradox has hit the ''baby boomers''—the generation now age 25–45. They want to retire earlier, began their families later, purchased their houses later, and carry larger consumer debt than their parents. As a result, most have less equity than their parents and are more dependent on employee benefits for retirement planning. Because of the high cost of their lifestyle, they find it difficult to put money into IRAs or salary-reduction savings plans. Recent changes in the tax law have reduced tax benefits available to working couples and single parents. However, other changes in the tax law allow for shorter pension vesting and greater portability of benefits from job to job.

Recognizing these changes, what can these employees do?

One strategy is to place all or a part of any cost-of-living increase into a salary-reduction savings plan (401K). This strategy is further enhanced if your company makes matching contributions on your behalf.

If you have made payroll deductions to purchase savings bonds, redirect these dollars into your company's salary-reduction savings plan. In general you will have a higher return, get the company match (if available), and incur no greater risk (assuming you invest in the plan's guaranteed principal and interest account).

If you seek growth, your company's stock is usually an available option.

Buying a home and making maximum use of your company tax-deferred savings plan are often your best investments for accumulating dollars and reducing taxes.

Many employees find it difficult to save any money because they have high monthly payments for cars, housing and major consumer goods. To free up more income for savings plans, consider using some consumer strategies presented in the pages ahead for:

- Using Credit
- Buying A Car
- Buying A Home

BUILDING GOOD CREDIT

Your Credit File: Timeliness Is A Virtue

It is essential these days to build a good credit record. Making late payments on installment loans or credit cards can haunt you for years. They can remain on your credit report for several years *after* you become current. Late payments on credit accounts can lead to credit line suspension and even stop you from securing credit in the future.

Credit defaults, charge-offs and judgments remain on your credit report for up to seven years from the date reported, even after you have paid your obligation. Bankruptcies normally destroy credit ratings.

Credit bureaus are not infallible. If you are denied credit, you are entitled to review your credit file report. Review it carefully. If there are errors, bring them to the attention of the bureau that issued the report, in writing.

In the event of divorce proceedings, learn who is to be responsible for which debt obligations and draft them into your divorce decree.

Ways To Build Good Credit:

- Own and use credit cards moderately. Paying them off in full in thirty days does not establish a payment record in all cases.
- Prepare a net worth/financial statement and keep it updated.
- Maintain a banking relationship with an institution that will work cooperatively with you. Your credit union can be such an institution.
- Be careful when co-signing loans for children, relatives, or friends. Co-signers are legally obligated for the debt and for timely payments—you could jeopardize your credit rating.
- Do not bite off more than you can chew. Credit cards today are readily available through the mail—use them judiciously.

CONSUMER STRATEGIES

RECOMMENDATION

Two guidelines on debt:

1. Finance only assets that have realistic potential to appreciate in value.
2. Pay cash or reduce debt on assets which are likely to depreciate in value.

For example, for major purchases, such as automobiles, home appliances and improvements, college education, etc., consider using home equity loans or refinancing the *whole* mortgage. The interest on these loans is tax deductible. Home equity loans have lower closing costs or loan origination fees than first mortgages. You should only refinance when interest rates are attractive and your equity is sizable.

TO LEASE OR TO BUY A CAR?

Given the increasing cost of automobiles, financing has become more complex. On high-priced cars, loans are often 5 years to ease the burden of heavy payments. Down payments are larger and interest is nondeductible. But, what is the auto worth at the end of the five-year term, particularly if the odometer reading exceeds 100,000 miles? These factors make auto leasing more attractive. Consider the following:

- On an auto lease, the down payment equals two monthly payments.
- Your loan amount is based on subtracting the ''book value'' at the end of the lease term (on a closed-end lease) from the current sales price (which you negotiate). For example, if the current sales price is $20,000 and the residual value (book value) is $10,000, your loan payment is based on only $10,000.
- You can put the difference between the lower lease payment and the loan payment, pretax, into your 401K. This will reduce your taxes and provide tax-deferred growth. Or you could put it in ''after tax'' and under certain conditions (and possible penalties), access it later if needed.
- If you want a new car every three or four years, leasing can be an effective way to go.
- You can always sell a car and pay off the lease if desired.
- You can usually roll to a new lease when your current lease is over.
- If you have a business, you can (within limits), deduct the lease as a business expense. See your accountant.
- At the end of your lease, you can get back your security deposit, give back the keys and walk away; or pay the residual and own the car.

What To Consider:

- Leases have restrictions on mileage, usually 15,000 per year. Over the maximum you pay about .06 per mile.
- You are responsible for normal maintenance and repairs not covered by the manufacturer's warranty.
- There are heavy penalties in some leases if you return the auto before the lease expires. Read the terms carefully; lease conditions vary by company.

RECOMMENDATION

When buying a car, use your credit union (when possible) and have payments payroll deducted. Buy a one- or two-year-old car. This could save 20 to 40 percent of the depreciation that a new car suffers. A one- or two-year-old car is often still covered by a factory warranty. An alternative strategy is to purchase older ''classic'' cars below book value and have them restored. These cars often hold their value or appreciate.

HYPOTHETICAL DEPRECIATION CURVE ON A GOOD-QUALITY AMERICAN CAR

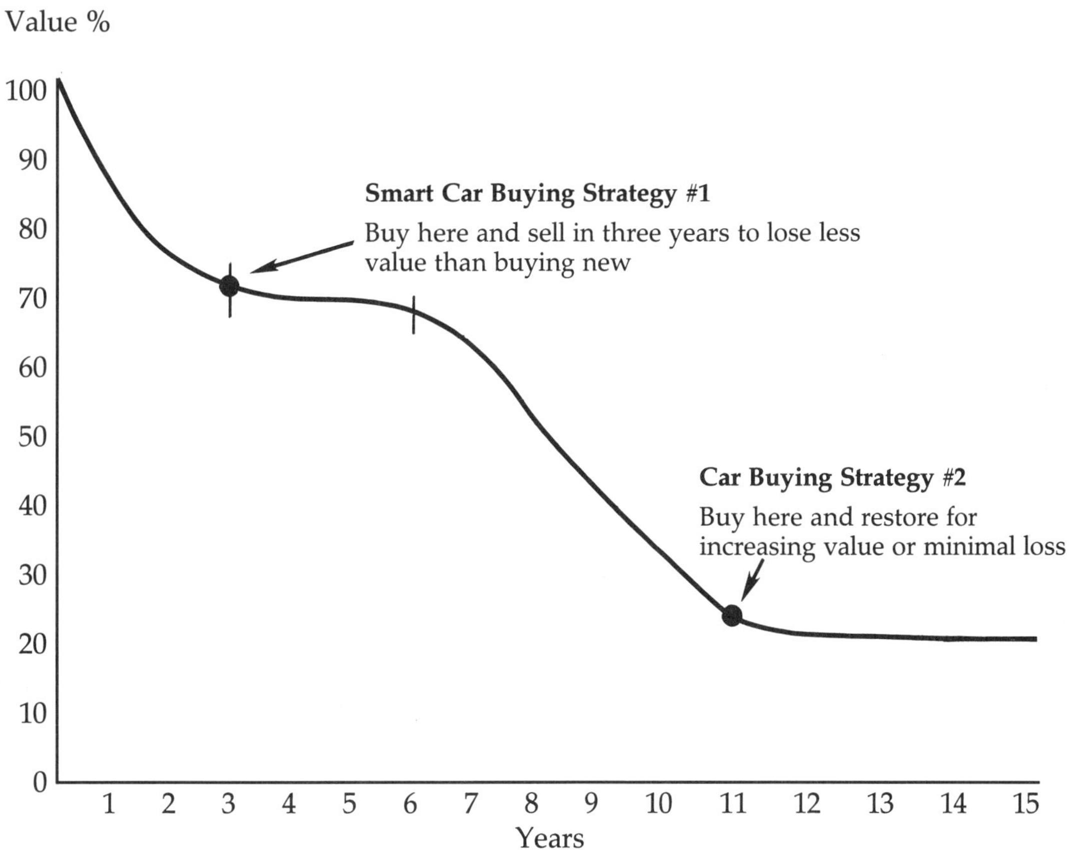

TO BUY OR TO RENT HOUSING?

Many employees of major corporations are familiar with two related terms: upward mobility and geographic mobility. Companies looking to promote talent internally move employees to other locations and absorb much of the cost. This normally includes:

- Moving costs.
- An agreement to buy an employee's home at *assessed* value if the employee can't sell it.
- Paying closing costs.

Under these circumstances, using a home to build wealth is a viable option.

In some cases, however, a geographic relocation may be for a year or two. Rather than sell a home and buy another and go through the process of securing a mortgage (not always at favorable interest rates), only to move again, you may consider renting a home as an alternative. For young people with little cash, no established credit, relatively high debt but great income potential—renting is a great option. You can rent a $200,000 house in many areas for $1,000 per month, ½% of market value. By comparison, purchasing the same home with a 20% down payment ($40,000), and a $160,000 mortgage at 10% interest for 30 years, would result in a monthly mortgage payment (P & I) of $1,404 (not to mention up to $7,000 in closing costs). If you invested the $40,000 home down payment at 10% and added the $400 difference between renting and buying, pretax to your 401K, you could have a better investment return and tax advantage through renting. You do have tax savings if you own because of mortgage interest deductions, but you can often rent with less monthly cost, even after tax savings.

Young singles, couples or families with limited cash who are committed to home purchase should consider creative financing. Strategies include:

- Renting with an option to buy (commonly ⅓ of rent applied to down payment).
- Arranging for the seller to carry a short term mortgage to balloon in 3, 4, or 5 years, which allows you time to obtain a mortgage.

Remember, owning *does not mean that:*

- Automatic tax savings are always greater than when renting.
- Your home will *definitely* appreciate in value.
- You will have more ''security'' than if you rent.

AGE 45–65: MIDDLE-AGE FINANCIAL DILEMMAS

A generation of people aged 45–65 are becoming affluent and achieving financial independence. This generation is in its peak earning years, and consequently in its peak tax-paying years. During these years, debt should be reduced and home equity increased. People are usually vested in their employee benefits program by this time. This group is most likely to initiate and maintain early retirement. Dual career families are not uncommon among this generation.

During these years there are often major financial dilemmas, including:

- An increasing percentage of income going to taxation because of the elimination of tax shelters and deductions.
- Less government help for children's education relative to the increased cost of education.
- Mergers and acquisitions that contribute to job instability, causing employees to change jobs—and benefits—more frequently.
- Retirement before age 62 which means no Social Security benefits until age 62, and reduced retirement benefits at that time.
- Dual career family interest in a partner's pension and retirement benefits. In this case financial planning requires insurance and investment assets to achieve long-term objectives.
- How to best use home equity to protect lifestyle and their retirement income.
- Early retirement may mean substantial lump-sum distributions from company-sponsored retirement plans, with tax consequences and penalties that require careful tax planning.

People in this generation have to make major decisions concerning lifestyle if they choose early retirement. Many who retire early tend to live active lifestyles that include extensive travel, active recreational activities, and major consumer purchases. If they are not careful with their assets, people in this group may have to return to work to maintain income to accommodate their buying power.

This group is often caught between dependent older children (cars, college, marriage) and the increasing dependence of aging parents (nurses, nursing home care, immobility).

SAVING FOR RETIREMENT

Because people are now living longer after retirement, Congress has realized the need to create tax incentives for individuals and corporations to accumulate larger pools of capital to be used for retirement.

These incentives currently include:

- Salary-reduction (pretax) savings plans, (some with matching company contributions). These are some of the best tax shelters available today and should be used to maximum advantage.
- Tax-deferred insurance policies and annuities.
- Tax-deferred company savings plans, employee stock option plans, incentive stock option plans, deferred compensation plans, and/or deferred bonus plans.
- Tax-deferred plans such as Simplified Employee Pensions (SEPs) and Individual Retirement Accounts (IRAs).
- Tax-favored treatment of profits realized on the sale of a personal residence and tax deductions for interest on home mortgages.

IT IS NEVER TOO EARLY TO BEGIN SAVING FOR RETIREMENT

RETIREMENT PLANNING DATES

Age	Retirement Event
50	Earliest possible retirement for some companies. You can join AARP. If you were 50 or older on January 1, 1986, you can use ten-year averaging on 401K withdrawal; otherwise use five-year averaging.
55	Early retirement at many companies. You can sell your residence with a lifetime exclusion of up to $125,000.
59½	You can withdraw lump sums from qualified retirement plans or tax-deferred annuities without incurring a 10 percent tax penalty.
62	You can receive reduced social security benefits.
65	You can receive full social security benefits.* You must pay Medicare surtax if your income tax is over $1,000.
70½	You can earn any amount without losing any social security. You must begin taxable withdrawals from all qualified retirement plans.

* The Social Security Amendment of 1983 increases the retirement age when unreduced benefits are available (presently age 65) by 2 months a year for workers reaching age 62 in 2000–2005; maintains age 66 for workers reaching age 62 in 2006–2016; increases by 2 months a year the retirement age for workers reaching age 62 in 2017–2022; and maintains age 67 for workers reaching age 62 after 2022 (i.e., reaching age 67 in 2027). The Normal Retirement Age for spouse's benefits moves upward in exactly the same way as that for workers; the Normal Retirement Age for widow(er)'s benefits also rises but in a slightly different manner (beginning for widow(er)s who attain age 60 in 2003 and reaching a Normal Retirement Age of 67 in 2029).

The 1983 amendments do not change the availability of reduced benefits at age 62 but revise the reduction factors so that there is further reduction (up to a maximum of 30% for workers entitled at age 62 after the retirement age is increased to age 67, rather than only up to 20% for entitlement at age 62 under current law).

EARLY RETIREMENT

Paradoxes seem to be part of human nature. We prepare ourselves and anxiously await a career with a great company. Then, once we begin work, we think about retirement! We can't wait to get in—and we can't wait to get out!

More workers are aspiring to retire earlier than age 65. This can create unique dilemmas which include:

- Many early retirees will receive reduced social security and retirement benefits.
- Early retirement does not necessarily mean not working. Many workers choose second or even third careers, and accumulate more retirement benefits along the way.
- Early retirees are more likely to have dependent children and/or dependent parents, which puts an extra strain on their financial resources.
- Persons retiring before age 62 cannot receive Social Security and may face tax penalties on withdrawals from IRAs and company benefit programs.

Many corporations today are realizing that offering early retirement as a form of down-sizing, through cash and benefits incentives can encourage skilled employees to leave that company and go to work for a competitor. As a result, some companies are reviewing the logic of early retirement policies aimed at employees between age 50 and 65.

PLANNING CAN MAKE YOUR RETIREMENT DREAMS COME TRUE

AGE 65–75: MAXIMUM BENEFIT RETIREE FINANCIAL DILEMMAS

The average retirement age for American workers has decreased in recent years to approximately age 59. Many workers now retire before age 65 because of an increase in accumulated assets, resulting from improvements in corporate tax-favored retirement programs, and/or from being part of a two-income household.

Those who retire at age 65 do have certain benefits that early retirees may not have, including:

- Working longer. If they planned properly, they will have accumulated more dollars in employee savings programs.
- Greater Social Security benefits. Ten years ago, 3 percent was the maximum contribution to Social Security. It was raised to 6.5 percent and now it is 7.51 percent. Those who currently work longer will have substantially more benefits when the last 33 years of contributions are averaged.
- More time as ''empty nesters''. This allows them to accumulate more personal net worth if they desire, because of lower household costs.

Retirees at age 65 are healthier, wealthier, and better prepared for retirement than any previous generation. . .but these blessings pose certain problems. A long, active retirement can strain resources, particularly if dependent children remain in the household or aging parents require care. A careful reconsideration of assets and early financial planning is needed to choose the best pension distribution option.

Upon retirement, people in this group may receive a large distribution from their retirement savings plan, possibly a pension lump-sum distribution. Tax planning in this case becomes essential, and should be started at least one year before retirement. Special tax reduction strategies may be available and asset repositioning is often advisable.

Retirees should ask an attorney to review their estate plan, including wills and trusts. Wealth-transference planning should be considered while both spouses are healthy.

Early planning can also help avoid a draining of assets should prolonged nursing-home care become necessary.

Retirees increasingly opt for new careers, primarily self-employment. Proper structuring of these new careers may produce tax savings and increased cash flow.

AGE 70½ AND BEYOND: SOME CONSIDERATIONS

At age 70½, the IRS requires (as of April 1, 1990) that IRA distributions and pension plan distributions must begin for those who reach age 70½ in 1989. There are no longer any restrictions placed on earnings which will affect Social Security benefits.

In later years, due to several factors which can include declining health, or possibly the loss of a spouse, there is a desire to settle into a secure, stable lifestyle. There tends to be less travel and fewer major purchases. This new emphasis often means a reallocation of assets to safer, more income-oriented investments. A move from the single-family dwelling to a full-service retirement community is increasingly common. Remaining nonliquid assets, such as the home, furniture, and collectibles, may be liquidated to maintain a comfortable lifestyle. Capital gains tax on the residence should be considered, particularly if the one-time exclusion of up to $125,000 has not been used on a prior sale of a personal residence.

Provisions must be made for the impact of inflation on the remaining estate. Many pension programs do not contain a cost-of-living provision. At a 6 percent inflation rate, the cost of living doubles every twelve years. In other words, with 6 percent inflation, the buying power of a fixed pension is halved every twelve years of retirement. The death of a spouse could further reduce income by reducing Social Security and/or pension payments. Planning for these experiences should begin prior to retirement and continue through the retirement years. Changes in the tax law, the economy and inflation rate should be constantly monitored and adjustments need to be made to protect retirement income and the estate.

A common goal for age 70 and beyond is for a life that is satisfying, relaxing, and trouble free. This goal can be achieved through the ongoing management of assets with the help of a financial planning team.

PART III

Employee Benefits

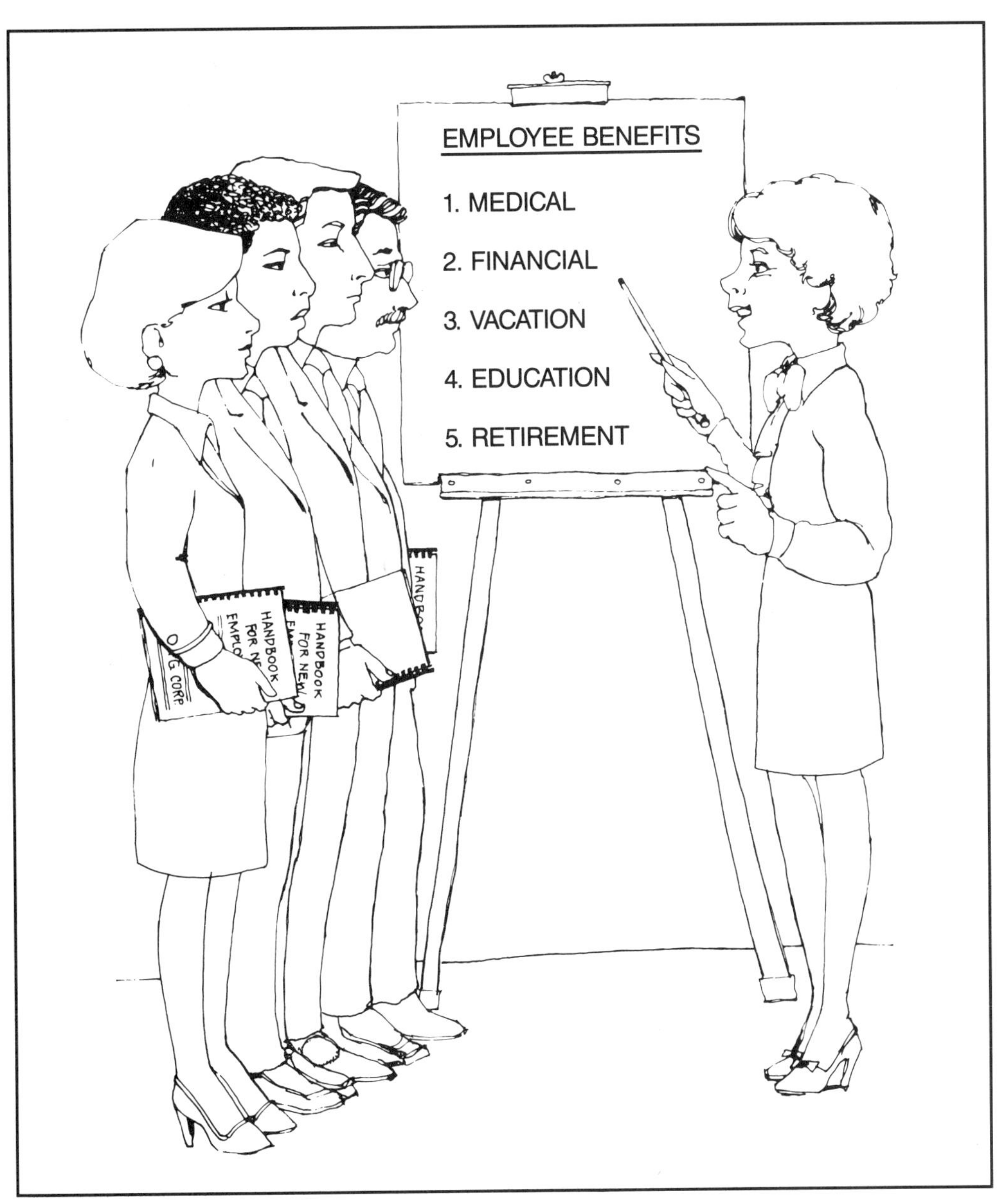

THE IMPORTANCE OF BENEFITS

Currently about 12 percent of the U.S. population, nearly 30 million persons, have retired and are over the age of 65. Retirement is occurring earlier and lasting longer. As the number of retirees grows, employee benefits packages are becoming the foundation of financial security. For many employees, tax-favored corporate benefits will replace Social Security as their primary source of income.

Inflation erodes the buying power of most personal assets. When this happens, benefits become more important. According to the 1988 Business Conditions Digest of the U.S. Department of Commerce, the consumer price index rose an average of 6.7 percent between 1967 and 1987. This means any purchase in 1967 would cost three times as much today! For example, the rising cost of education can eat into personal assets that once would have been used for retirement planning.

Faced with the need to protect and increase retirement assets, employee benefits are more important than ever before.

Employees do not always, however:

- Understand their benefit programs.
- Know how to use a benefits programs effectively.
- Know how to integrate these programs with financial planning.

LEARN ABOUT YOUR BENEFITS

Benefits can enhance your lifestyle. Often they are worth more than 25 percent of your salary! But you have to know how they work and how to obtain information about them. Many benefits are elective. This means you must ask for them or sign up for them. You can't just assume that they are automatically in force.

There are some primary sources of information about your benefits. These include:

1. Your employer's personnel department which may provide:
   - Orientation programs for new employees.
   - Formal classes or meetings about pay and benefits.
   - Individual counseling sessions with staff members trained to handle compensation questions.
2. Employee benefits manuals and annual statements concerning the value of the benefits and the rules on how to use them.
3. If you belong to a labor union you can learn about your benefits from your union leadership.

RECOMMENDATION

Don't rely on fellow workers to advise you about your benefits. Each worker has a different package of pay and benefits. Only your employer can adequately inform you about what benefits are available and how they work for you.

To stay informed about your benefits, follow these steps:

1. Keep all pay and benefits manuals as they are given to you.
2. Keep your annual benefit statements and any updated manuals given you by your employer in a safe place.
3. Pay attention to benefits announcements by your employer so you can act in time to make a choice about options.
4. Get the name and telephone number of the person responsible for explaining benefits. When in doubt, consult that person.

To make the most of your benefits—make yourself knowledgeable about them and keep current on any changes to them.

BENEFITS CHECKLIST

TYPE OF BENEFIT	DO I HAVE THIS?	CAN I GET THIS?	DO I KNOW HOW THIS WORKS?
1. Pay-Oriented Benefits			
Inflation-adjusted increasing pay scale			
Incentive bonuses for productivity			
Profit-sharing bonuses			
Overtime pay for extra work			
2. Insurance-Oriented Benefits			
Co-paid health insurance			
Employer-paid health ins. for family			
Employee supplemental life ins.			
Employer-paid life ins. for family			
Employer-paid short-term disability ins.			
Employer-paid long-term disability ins.			
Paid dental care			
Paid dental care for family			
Paid eye care			
Paid eye care for family			
Payroll-deduction auto ins.			
3. Savings-Oriented Benefits			
U.S. Savings bond purchase plan			
Credit unions			
4. Investment-Oriented Benefits			
Employee stock ownership plan			
Incentive stock option plan			
5. Retirement-Oriented Benefits			
Salary-reduction savings plans 401K or 403B			
Employer partially matches your savings plan contribution			
Deferred compensation bonus plan			
Retirement pension plan			

BENEFITS CHECKLIST (Continued)

TYPE OF BENEFIT	DO I HAVE THIS?	CAN I GET THIS?	DO I KNOW HOW THIS WORKS?
Full & Supplemental Health care after retirement			
6. Lifestyle Benefits			
Paid vacation time	days		
Family or maternity leave			
Paid sick days	days		
Unused sick days can be taken as cash bonus on retirement			
Travel benefits paid by employer			
Daycare center at work			
Recreational facilities at work			
Use of company outdoor facilities			
7. Employee Development Benefits			
Educational benefits			
Educational benefits for family			
Financial planning education			
Psychiatric or marital counseling			
Moving expenses paid by employer			
Relocation services & counseling			
Home purchase by employer if not sold			
Pre-retirement education			
Fitness education			
Pre-paid legal services			
8. Other Benefits			
Employer loan or salary advance			
______________			
______________			

TYPES OF BENEFITS

In the checklist on pages 36–37, the benefits were arranged in seven groups. Let's look at each group in more detail.

1. PAY-ORIENTED BENEFITS

Strictly speaking, pay is considered compensation, and not a benefit.

Ask your personnel representative about what incentives are offered and how to obtain them. More and more companies are using pay incentives to stimulate productivity.

2. INSURANCE-ORIENTED BENEFITS

Insurance is typically the first benefit employees name. This is often the largest area of all employee benefits and the most expensive. In the past, many employers paid all costs, but increasingly some program costs are shared between the employer and the employee.

Cafeteria Plans or flexible benefit plans offer everything from a special account to pay certain bills for employees, to multiple-choice health, life, and disability plans, to savings plans. Most of these plans are offered on a pretax basis. The employee is given a specific amount of money to spend on the benefits he or she wants. Both the company and the employee save on taxes. If your cafeteria plan is funded by the company, participate to maximum benefit. (Note that from January 1, 1990, unused dollars must remain in the plan.) The ultimate value of these benefit programs is determined by your tax bracket and the benefit pricing.

The choices are many, so choose carefully. There are trade-offs. Disability benefits are taxable if premium payments are made pretax. Life insurance coverage may become imputed income if premiums are pretax, and certain health plan benefits may be taxable. It is advisable to consult with a personnel representative to insure you completely understand your options.

In the next few pages, specific insurance benefits will be examined in detail.

TYPES OF BENEFITS (Continued)

Health Insurance

Employees often have a choice of health care programs.

The two most common are the PPO (Preferred Provider Organization) and the HMO (Health Maintenance Organization).

PPOs are generally part of an indemnity medical plan. The employee is reimbursed for a percentage of his or her payments to physicians, hospitals, pharmacies, and laboratories. There is a maximum out-of-pocket expense, and usually a fixed deductible each year. Employees receive a higher level of reimbursement from the plan if they use a preferred provider rather than a nonpreferred provider. PPO plans often cover emergency room payment without any deductible. Many have optional dental care, cancer care, eye care, and/or low- or no-cost prescription service supplements. These options may or may not cost the employee an additional premium. Family members can normally be included in PPOs for free or at a favorable rate.

HMOs offer preventive medicine, ''well care,'' and a low fixed payment ($10 to $20 on average) for each office visit or hospital stay.

Pros and Cons

PPOs allow you to use a physician or facility of your choice. The insurance carrier will first deduct your annual deductible and then pay a percentage, usually 75 to 100 percent, of ''the usual and customary charges.''

PPOs can be expensive for the employee because of:

- High cost
- High deductibles
- High co-payments

HMOs offer preventive medicine, such as a full annual physical checkup. They are relatively inexpensive, but you are limited to the physicians on the list provided by your employer's health carrier. You may even have to use specific hospitals.

Some standard limitations of HMOs are:

- The doctors and facilities are sometimes far from the employee's home or office, or from children's schools.
- You generally need approval for medical attention when out of town.
- There may be a poor selection of physicians.

TYPES OF BENEFITS (Continued)

Disability Insurance

Most employee benefit packages offer short- and long-term group plans for income continuation in the case of illness or disability.

Short-term disability coverage usually provides full salary for up to one year depending on your employment level, years of service, and your company plan.

Long-term disability coverage picks up where short-term coverage ends, typically providing up to 60 percent of an employee's base wage until that employee reaches age 65.

In general, group disability benefits are coordinated with workman's compensation, your pension disability program, and Social Security disability coverage. Additional provisions may include:

- A cost of living provision annually adjusted, which can increase monthly indemnity payments by 4 to 7 percent.
- A lifetime benefit provision.
- An increased benefit option, if the employee is not eligible for Social Security disability payments.
- A reduced monthly indemnity allowing part-time return to work.

RECOMMENDATION

Some studies indicate that up to 80 percent of all Social Security disability claims are disallowed. So don't count on them! You may want to purchase additional supplement insurance in case you become disabled. The probability of a disability during your lifetime is statistically significant. Ask your company's insurance carrier or your benefits officer about supplemental coverage.

TYPES OF BENEFITS (Continued)

Life Insurance

Usually group term life insurance will be provided by your employer through separate coverage. Sometimes this will be as part of your health care or even part of your savings plan. This benefit may also include an accidental death and dismemberment provision doubling the death benefit. Many firms offer payroll deducted supplemental life insurance from one to four times your base salary. You can also purchase minimal amounts of family coverage at favorable rates.

RECOMMENDATION

For employees 40 to 45 years of age, supplemental group term insurance is generally a good buy. Younger workers may be able to find a better value on their own. Remember, life insurance is not just to pay for burial or pay off bills in the event of an employee's death. It also should provide a continued income to dependents, and protect assets of the estate. Under current law the insurance death benefit passes to listed beneficiaries free of income tax.

For a family of four, the primary income earner should carry a minimum of $250,000 death benefit exclusive of accidental death provisions. Because group coverage could lapse due to early retirement, a career change, prolonged job search, or termination of employment, a whole life insurance policy should be purchased. This can be a good investment as well as financial protection at death, but a careful analysis by a qualified financial planner is necessary to establish cost and internal rate of return. A whole life contract can also increase your retirement pension income if it's selected and applied properly. (This concept called pension maximization will be discussed in Chapter 6.)

TYPES OF BENEFITS (Continued)

3. SAVINGS-ORIENTED BENEFITS

Many employers help employees save money easily with automatic payroll deductions. Savings are not just for long-term goals like retirement. They also help you set aside a little bit each pay period for vacations, college expenses, buying a car or a house, or building an emergency fund. These savings plans may be tax-favored or not.

4. INVESTMENT-ORIENTED BENEFITS

Investment plans involve longer holding periods than savings plans. They normally involve less liquidity and more risk. But they can give higher rates of return than savings plans and provide tax deferral of earnings over the holding period. The rules can be complex and the investment choices can vary widely. You will need to consult your tax and investment advisors as well as your benefits officers about how to best use these plans. The most common investment-oriented plans are:

- *Employee Stock Ownership Plans (ESOP).* The company makes the contribution, or may allow employees to buy company stock at or below market prices, with little or no commission costs. If the company stock is a good investment, these plans can build wealth. But if the company stock performs poorly, employees could lose money by participating. Consult your investment advisor about the advantages of buying your company stock.
- *Incentive Stock Options (ISO).* These are commonly used for rewarding managers or top-level employees for special services or high productivity. ISOs are generally tax deferred, but they may be subject to holding period requirements and other restrictions before they can be exercised at set prices.

TYPES OF BENEFITS (Continued)

5. RETIREMENT-ORIENTED BENEFITS

There are three main retirement benefits: government pension benefits, company pension plans, and deferred compensation plans. We'll look at each individually:

A. Social Security

All employees in the United States must pay into the Social Security system if they earn more than a few hundred dollars a year. The employer is required by law to deduct these contributions (7.51 percent of compensation up to $48,000 in 1989) and to pay a matching contribution of 7.51 percent of the employee's compensation. This 15 percent tax on compensation goes into the national budget and is used to pay benefits to people already retired. The system was restructured in the early 1980s to build a surplus of funds for the ''baby boom'' generation when they start to retire.

Social Security benefits start as early as age 62 and provide 80 percent of the full benefit available to retirees at age 65. The benefit is really a life annuity that is adjusted for inflation each year if inflation exceeds 3 percent.

This benefit pays (on average) between one-fourth and one-third of what a retiree needs to preserve his or her lifestyle, and, therefore, may need to be supplemented with additional sources of retirement income.

Social Security benefits are currently tax free to retirees who earn a modified adjusted income of less than $25,000 if single, or $32,000 if married. People with incomes over that amount can have up to half of their benefit subject to income taxes.

Calculation of Social Security benefits are complex. They are based on age, salary history, and occupational sector. Consult your tax planner or the Social Security office to determine your benefit.

To understand your benefits you can contact your local office of the Social Security Administration for a free consultation and statement of your benefits. The current maximum monthly income available to a single employee who has contributed the maximum tax for forty years, is just over $900 per month at age 65.

B. Company Pension Plans

Pension plans are offered to employees by a variety of companies, large and small. Plan structures vary widely in detail and are governed by a host of government regulations. Most plans pay a regular monthly income to employees and their spouses upon retirement. The length of service required for vesting has been reduced as a result of tax law changes. Pensions are more portable than ever. Over the next several decades employees will accumulate portfolios of retirement benefits. They will need advice from employers and tax and investment advisors to protect and enjoy these complex and valuable benefits.

TYPES OF BENEFITS (Continued)

C. Deferred Compensation Plans

These plans are designed to augment pension and Social Security income after retirement. They can be used for financial goals other than retirement. In CODAs (Cash or Deferred Arrangements) an employer's plan may permit up to 25% of compensation contribution. These plans vary in structure. They generally allow employees to have some salary deducted each pay period and deposited into a savings or investment vehicle for future use. There are several types of deferred compensation plans, depending on the type of employer: 401K plans or PSPs, 403B plans or TSAs, 457 plans, SEP-IRA plans, and IRAs. We'll look at each individually.

1. *401K or Salary Deferral Plans* are tax-deferred retirement savings plans governed by section 401K of the tax code. They allow employees to have some salary deducted before or after taxes and invested in a company plan. The plan may offer a combination of investment choices: the company stock, a guaranteed fixed savings account, or various types of mutual funds.

Employees can elect to reduce taxable salary by contributing to these plans. The rules vary from company to company. The IRS guidelines allow a maximum contribution of 25 percent of salary up to an inflation-adjusted limit ($7,627 in 1989). In reality, the company plan may only allow smaller amounts to be contributed. Consult your 401K plan manual or employee benefits advisors about your contribution levels.

After-tax contributions can also be made to these plans. Many companies sweeten their plans by matching the employees' contribution up to a specified amount.

Salary deferral plans may allow financial hardship withdrawals, in the form of loans for major financial exigencies such as a death in the family, health care emergencies, college tuition, or the buying of a primary residence. This is true only if you exhaust all other sources of income. Withdrawals are taxable as income and are likely to incur a 10% penalty. Loans are not taxable, but must be paid back within a stated period (typically 5 years unless it is for home purchase) at stated interest rate. Also loans are severely restricted ($50,000 or less) under current law.

RECOMMENDATION

401K plans can grow very rapidly if employers make matching contributions and investment performance is good. If you plan to leave the money in the plan for more than two or three years, it is generally best to contribute the maximum that you can afford on a before-tax rather than an after-tax basis. Even though there can be taxes and a 10 percent tax penalty for early withdrawal before age 59½, the tax deferral, matching contribution, and investment performance will often leave you ahead of other types of taxable investment plans or of the after-tax contribution method.

TYPES OF BENEFITS (Continued)

2. *403 B Plans or Tax-Sheltered Annuities (TSAs)* are payroll-deducted, tax-deferred savings plans available to employees of nonprofit organizations such as school systems and churches. Section 403B of the tax code governs the taxation of these plans. The plan investment options vary from employer to employer but generally offer a package of mutual funds or variable annuities. Contributions to the plan can reduce salary and thus taxable income, making these plans attractive tax shelters. The employer may not make matching contributions but the plans allow special preretirement ''catch-up'' contributions and higher levels of contributions than the 401K plans. Employees can contribute up to 20 percent of salary or $9,500 annually as a maximum.

Employee contributions are 100 percent vested and can be rolled to IRAs without tax if you change employers.

3. *457 Plans or Nonqualified, Deferred Compensation Programs* are available to employees of city or state governments or agencies. Because they are nonqualified they can not be rolled to an IRA. Consult your advisors on the similarities and differences and the pros and cons of these plans.

RECOMMENDATION

Although employees of nonprofit organizations do not often get matching contributions in their deferred compensation plans, there are still some advantages to using the 403B and 457 plans:

- Taxable income can be reduced.
- Investment performance can be excellent and is tax-deferred until money is withdrawn.
- It is easy to contribute to the plans and the preretirement catch-up provisions may enable peak wage earners to deposit large amounts of money during the last few years before retirement.

TYPES OF BENEFITS (Continued)

4. *Simplified Employee Pension Individual Retirement Accounts (SEP-IRAs)* are tax-deferred retirement accounts set up by sole proprietors or small employers who do not have any other type of retirement plan. They are "simple" pension plans because there are fewer record-keeping and reporting requirements relative to other retirement plans.

The employer can contribute up to $30,000 or 15 percent of compensation. Whatever percentage the employer elects must be offered to employees. Employees may contribute up to $2000 per year in lieu of their IRA contributions.

If you terminate employment, you may roll your plan dollars into another IRA without tax. All employer contributions are immediately 100% vested.

Withdrawals from the plan before age 59½ face the same taxes and tax penalties that govern other plans. Participation may still be a good idea because taxable salary is reduced and money is being saved for future use in retirement.

5. *Individual Retirement Accounts (IRAs)* are not company-sponsored plans. Any individual who received salary or personal service income up to age 70½ may contribute. The maximum IRA contribution is 100% of salary up to $2,000 each year. This is independent of other retirement plans or deferred compensation plans.

Single employees earning less than $34,000 adjusted gross income may deduct part of their IRA contribution from their taxable income; if they earn less than $25,000, they may deduct all of the contribution. Married couples filing jointly may deduct part of the contribution if they earn less than $50,000 and all of the contribution if they earn less than $40,000. These rules apply to employees who are participants in employer-sponsored retirement plans. If not a participant in one of these plans, then the entire IRA contribution is deductible, regardless of income levels.

IRA monies can be invested in a wide variety of financial investments, but there are some restrictions.

TYPES OF BENEFITS (Continued)

6. *Deferred Compensation Plan Investment Guideline*
Many retirement plans offer a wide variety of investment choices to employees, including:

- Fixed-interest and guaranteed-principal investments
- Money market accounts
- Government or corporate bond mutual funds
- Stock mutual funds
- Company stock

To make choices effectively, you should gather information from your benefits advisors on the investment alternatives and then consult with an investment advisor about the best alternatives for you. Your personnel and benefits advisors are generally not permitted to make investment suggestions and expect you to make the choice and bear the consequences.

Some general investment guidelines:

- Younger employees should have some, if not all, of their money invested in growth investments such as stock or stock mutual funds. Over many years, stocks tend to grow in value faster than bonds or fixed-interest accounts.
- More conservative investors or investors entering middle age may wish to balance their investment portfolios, half in high-interest-bearing accounts and half in stocks and bonds for a more secure growth and income performance.
- Employees nearing retirement age need to protect principal and profits from market risks. They could consider placing most, if not all, of their funds into those accounts with guaranteed principal and interest.
- Your situation may vary from these guidelines, so you must decide with your advisors what mix of investments is appropriate for you.
- All plans allow some flexibility in making changes, but be warned that these are not trading accounts. Making a change usually takes time and requires written instructions to your benefits department. To avoid delays, you should know the rules and procedures before making any changes.

TYPES OF BENEFITS (Continued)

6. LIFESTYLE BENEFITS

Many companies offer a variety of fringe benefits to enrich or enhance employees lifestyles. Some of these benefits are financial and some are not. Some may be included as taxable income.

These benefits can enrich life on the job by creating a sense of belonging to a wider ''Corporate Culture.'' They generally enhance employee morale, loyalty, and productivity.

Lifestyle benefits include:

- Day care centers at work
- Recreational facilities
- Sport/hobby organizations sponsored by employers
- Paid vacation time
- Sick leave
- Family or maternity leave
- Paid holidays
- Food services on site at reduced prices

7. EMPLOYEE DEVELOPMENT BENEFITS

Many employers now offer a variety of educational and counseling services such as:

- Employee assistance programs, dealing with a variety of personal issues such as alcohol or drug abuse, marital problems, emotional crises, etc.
- Relocation services
- Tuition reimbursement programs
- Company-paid educational courses on the job or in a college of your choice.
- Employee financial education and planning services

CONCLUSION—EMPLOYER BENEFITS

Employers across the nation spend billions of dollars each year to provide a wide range of benefits to their employees. But even the best benefit package must be used properly to be effective. It is the employee's responsibility to do the reading, ask the questions, and select and use the benefits. Knowledge is profit for the employee who takes the time to become informed.

PART IV

Cash Management and Tax Reduction

CASH MANAGEMENT

Many employees wonder where the dollars will come from to invest in their benefit programs. To produce the necessary dollars, it is necessary to first isolate those dollars through a cash management system.

Many Americans don't manage their money—they let their money manage them. When we save, it is usually for something we already want or need. Europeans and Asians save first (about 18 percent of their income) and then pay their monthly expenses. Their saving is not for spending, it is to accumulate wealth. Americans have had less inflation than the Japanese, Taiwanese or Europeans. We rank about 15th in cost of living and 8th in standard of living. We have the highest average income per capita. So we are in a perfect position to save as much as, or more than, our foreign counterparts. In fact, we save far less of our disposable income. Obviously, savings depends on attitude, not just on income.

To save money, an orderly system of cash management is required. Begin your system by prioritizing your uses of cash as follows:

- Mortgages: principal and interest
- Property taxes and insurance
- Home maintenance and utilities
- Auto expenses: gas, maintenance, insurance, tags
- Charge accounts and personal loans
- Insurance costs: health, life, disability, liability
- Health costs: deductibles, out of pocket expense, prescriptions, glasses, dental
- Food, clothing, entertainment expenses
- Gifts
- Vacations: weekends and annual trips
- Education expenses
- Charitable donations
- Miscellaneous expenses—including raids on the ATM at your local bank

ITEMIZE YOUR MONTHLY EXPENSES

The next step is to itemize monthly income sources. Then sort out monthly from periodic expenses—such as those paid quarterly or at other intervals. Your net monthly income should exceed monthly expenses. The remaining dollar total should exceed periodic expenses. When all your expenses have been met, the remaining money is discretionary income that is available for savings and/or investment.

Here is a simple cash management system to separate savings and cash reserves from monthly cash flow.

- All net monthly income goes into a separate interest-bearing account, such as a government-insured money market account, a credit union, or an interest-bearing checking account.
- A monthly withdrawal is then made equal to your monthly expenses and deposited in your regular checking account for distribution.
- The remainder from the day you get paid is earning interest in your money market account. Pay your expenses as they become due. The rest is savings.

Remember savings is a disciplined decision, not a financial accident. Use this system, and you'll have great results.

The best thing about employee savings plans and profit sharing plans is that you can elect to save first, rather than last, by enrolling in payroll deduction programs. This not only makes saving easy and automatic, but can also help reduce income taxes and costs associated with buying investments.

A CASH MANAGEMENT PLAN

Convenience and Control of Your Money

Deposit all income in a government-insured money market account; withdraw for monthly and periodic needs. The balance of your cash should be directed to your 5 KEY FINANCIAL PRIORITIES.

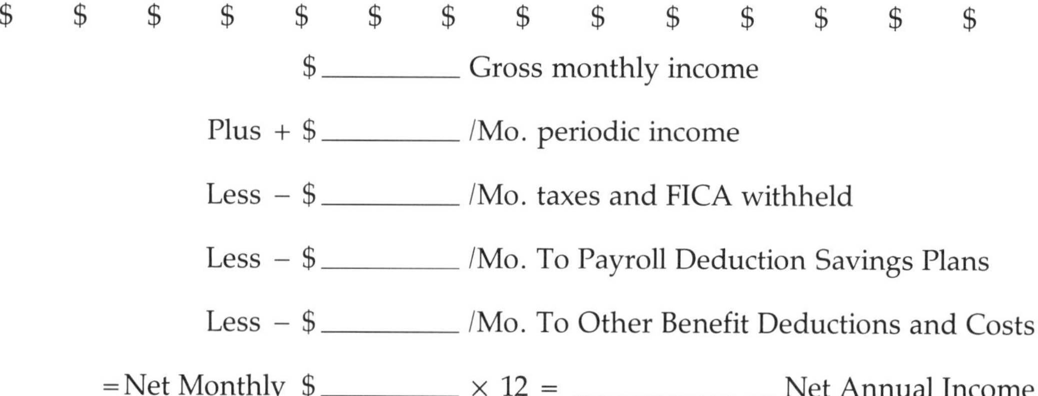

$ $ $ $ $ $ $ $ $ $ $ $ $ $

$_________ Gross monthly income

Plus + $_________ /Mo. periodic income

Less – $_________ /Mo. taxes and FICA withheld

Less – $_________ /Mo. To Payroll Deduction Savings Plans

Less – $_________ /Mo. To Other Benefit Deductions and Costs

=Net Monthly $_________ × 12 = _____________ Net Annual Income

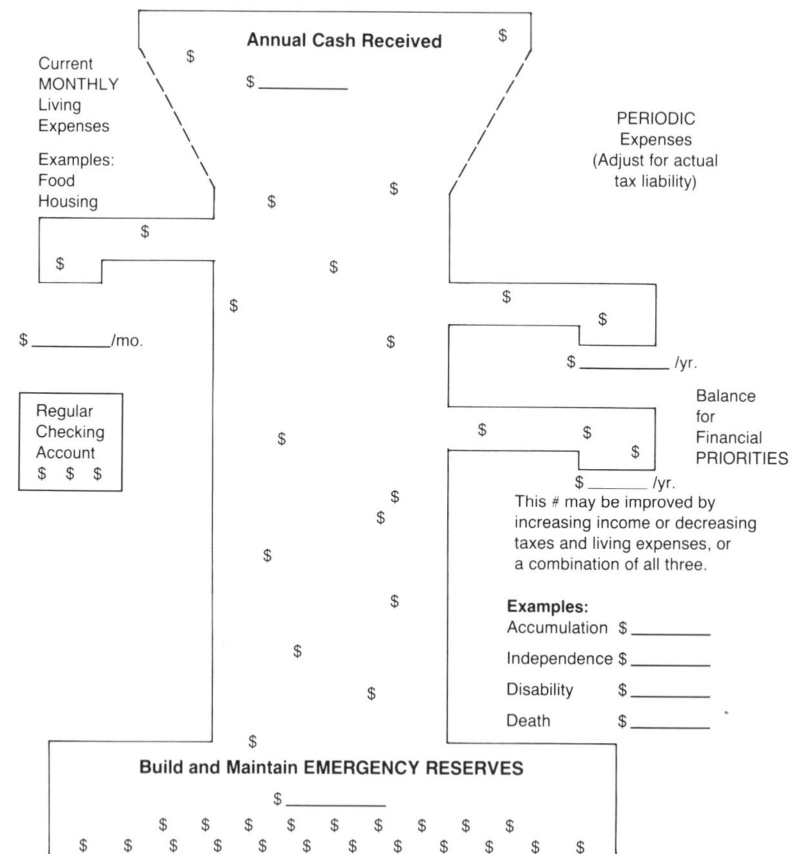

TAX REDUCTION

Paying Only What You Owe

Our tax system is a *net income tax system.* This means that you may use every legal means to reduce net taxable income. The tax system is so complex that many taxpayers seek professional advice about reducing their tax liability. Legal tax avoidance through careful planning and use of the law is smart and can yield sizable tax savings. Tax evasion, however, is illegal and can get you five to ten years in a federal prison.

Learn To Use Tax Advisors

Tax advisors are: certified public accountants, agents enrolled with the IRS or attorneys trained in tax law.

Other sources for tax planning information are:

- Financial planners
- Investment advisors
- Bankers/trust officers
- Real estate professionals
- Insurance agents
- Business consultants

Accountants are the most qualified advisors to *prepare* an accurate tax return and to review investment strategies.

Financial planners are most qualified to *develop strategies* for tax reduction, tax-favored investing, retirement planning, and estate planning.

Careful tax planning can save hundreds or thousands of dollars, year after year. The less tax you are legally required to pay, the more money you will have for funding company savings plans or other investments.

To reduce your taxes:

- Become familiar with the tax system and how it affects your situation.
- Keep accurate records.
- Prepare a preliminary tax projection with a tax advisor each year.
- Maximize personal deductions, exemptions, and credits.
- Structure the flow of your income.
- Use tax-favored investments.
- Use tax-favored employee benefits.
- Invest in business ventures and real estate.

The rest of Part IV is devoted to a detailed look at nine tax-reduction strategies.

NINE TAX REDUCTION STRATEGIES

1. USE SALARY-REDUCTION SAVINGS PLANS

The tax code identifies three types of salary-reduction savings plans (discussed in Part III):

401K plans for employees of profit-making public corporations

403B plans for employees of nonprofit organizations

457 plans—nonqualified deferred compensation

SEE NEXT PAGE
FOR A 401K EXAMPLE

SALARY REDUCTION SAVINGS PLANS

401K ILLUSTRATION

John wants to reduce his income taxes.

John earns $30,000 a year and his wife earns $10,000. They are in the 28 percent tax bracket.

John has an IRA to which he can contribute $2,000 but he wants to put more than that away for retirement.

He finds that his company offers a 401K plan which invests in a family of mutual funds as well as in the company's stock. The company will make matching 50% contributions up to 6 percent of his salary.

John asks his payroll department to withhold 15 percent of his salary to contribute to the 401K plan.

John can still contribute to his IRA, thus putting away $6,500 of his annual income—all tax deductible under current law.

In a 28 percent tax bracket these two strategies will reduce his income taxes in 1989 by $1,820. This is serious money!

John's taxable salary is reduced by	$4,500
Company matches fifty cents on the dollar up to 6% of his salary, adding	$ 900
The $5,400 earns 10%, tax deferred	$ 540
Tax savings	$1,820
John's investment of $4,500 is worth in one year John gets a spectacular return of 72 percent in the first year—all tax deferred	$7,760

If John has an emergency, he may be able to borrow his funds out of the plan without a 10 percent withdrawal tax penalty of an IRA. There are severe IRS restrictions on borrowing, however, Congress is currently considering several uses of IRA and qualified plan money for first time home purchases under certain restrictions.

If John can't afford to contribute to both the 401K plan and the IRA, he should still contribute to the 401K to get the company matching funds.

401K ILLUSTRATION

GETTING THE MOST FROM YOUR 401K WHEN YOU CONTRIBUTE BEFORE TAX TO REDUCE TAXABLE INCOME

Here is a hypothetical illustration of the total return on a $1 contribution in a 401K where the company matches 50%. In this hypothetical illustration the return is an astounding 65% on your $1—and you have *no* risk.

$ 1.00	CONTRIBUTION OF YOUR MONEY TO MATCHING 401K. YOU KEEP .28, NOT THE GOVERNMENT. YOU HAVE A WHOLE DOLLAR.
+ .50	COMPANY CONTRIBUTION TO YOUR PLAN
+ .15	EARNINGS ON THE MONEY AT 10% RATE TAX DEFERRED (Rate Varies)
$ 1.65	IN TOTAL SAVINGS
– 1.00	CONTRIBUTION OF YOUR MONEY
.65	65% EARNED IN FIRST YEAR SAVINGS

Even if you have to withdraw money before you reach age 59½ and have to pay a 10% tax penalty, plus tax on the withdrawal, the tax-deferred growth and company match still make the 401K plan one of the best ways to reduce taxes while accumulating capital automatically with little or no cost.

NINE TAX REDUCTION STRATEGIES (Continued)

2. USE IRAs

IRAs are now a ''last stand'' tactic. Use an IRA after maximizing your deferred savings plan contribution. Annual IRA deductions for married persons are phased out between $40,000 and $50,000 adjusted gross income; for singles it is phased out between $25,000 and $35,000. Regardless of deductibility, every working person can make an annual IRA contribution of $2,000 and enjoy tax-deferred growth. You can make your contribution for the previous tax year up to April 15th.

The most flexible IRAs are the Self-Directed Individual Retirement Accounts offered by investment firms. Self-directed IRA's are flexible because:

- They allow you to invest in a wide range of qualified investments while having only one custodial account.
- They can ease record keeping by consolidating scattered IRAs into one self-directed portfolio.
- Large amounts of money rolled into an IRA may benefit from the investment diversification available from the self-directed IRA.

Consult your financial advisors on the various alternatives.

NINE TAX REDUCTION STRATEGIES (Continued)

3. USE THE HOME AS A TAX SHELTER AND BANK

You may deduct the interest and taxes you pay on your primary residence and a secondary home.

Home equity debt that does not exceed the home's fair market value reduced by the amount of acquisition indebtedness up to $100,000 generates fully deductible interest costs.

Your home equity can be used to pay off other personal debt (car loans, credit card loans, personal loans) which otherwise would not be fully deductible.

People who have attained the age of 55 can elect a onetime exclusion of up to $125,000 of the gain from the sale of their principal residence.

RISKS OF USING YOUR HOME AS A BANK

- Refinancing a home may have considerable costs.
- Sufficient income is required to pay house payments on time or you could lose your home.
- It may generate an alternative minimum tax problem.

REWARDS OF USING YOUR HOME AS A BANK

- The equity value of your home is an excellent financial resource for meeting large life-cycle expenses like college education, major investment opportunities, wedding costs, retirement income.
- Major equipment purchases such as cars, boats, or major appliances can be paid for with cash from a home equity loan or new mortgage. It is hoped that when the equipment must be replaced, your home equity will have increased enough to meet new costs.
- The first and second home provide an excellent way to accumulate assets. At the same time, these assets provide a lot of personal pleasure and satisfaction.
- Having a mortgage provides relief from tax payments. It is sometimes beneficial, even in retirement.

See your tax advisor before making any major decisions about using your home as a tax shelter.

4. USE TAX-FAVORED INTEREST ON SAVINGS

If you have more than a few months' salary in taxable savings and money market accounts, you should consider tax-favored savings and investment vehicles. Several are listed below:

Investments that are free of federal income tax:

- Individual municipal bonds
- Municipal bond unit investment trusts
- Municipal bond mutual funds
- Tax-free money market funds investing in municipal short-term notes

Note that capital gains realized on sale, maturity or call of municipal bonds, trusts and funds are subject to income tax. Also, municipal bonds can have market, interest rate risks, and other adverse tax features, so consult your financial and tax advisors before investing.

Investments that defer income tax on interest or gains until withdrawal or sale:

- U.S. government series E savings bonds
- Tax-deferred annuities, fixed and variable
- Growth stocks that pay no dividends
- Cash value life insurance policies such as:
  Whole life
  Universal life
  Universal variable life
  Single premium whole life
- Tangible assets (gold, art, real estate) held for investment purposes.

BUFORD AND WILHELMINA—AN EXAMPLE

WHY TAX CONTROL?

Buford and Wilhelmina invest $100,000 in two investments: one is taxable, one is tax-controlled. They are in the 33 percent tax bracket (it makes math easier) and each investment yields 9 percent.

	TAXABLE	TAX-CONTROLLED
Yield	9%	9%
Tax Bracket	−33%	−0%
After-tax yield	6%	9%

Using the Rule of 72 to find out how long it would take for money to double...

TAXABLE	TAX-CONTROLLED
72 divided by 6 = 12 In 12 years the investment would grow to $200,000. In 24 years to $400,000.	72 divided by 9 = 8 In 8 years the investment would grow to $200,000. In 16 years to $400,000. In 24 years to $800,000.

If Buford and Wilhelmina paid the tax in the tax-controlled account and made a full withdrawal 24 years later, it would look like this:

	TAXABLE	TAX-CONTROLLED
Amount after 24 years	$400,000	$800,000
Original investment	−100,000	−100,000
Increase	$300,000	$700,000
Tax due at 33%	− 0	−220,000
Net increase after tax	$300,000	$480,000

The tax-controlled growth is $180,000 net gain over a fully taxable investment. Here are 180,000 reasons to use tax control.

If Buford and Wilhelmina retired and wanted to draw monthly income from their investments, it would look like this:

	TAXABLE	TAX-CONTROLLED
At 8 percent	$2,666 a month, taxable	$5,333 a month, taxable

Over a 24-year accumulation period, Buford and Wilhelmina can draw out twice as much income using tax control compared to a taxable investment.

By the way, Buford and Wilhelmina can have as much safety in the tax-controlled investment as in the taxable investment.

NINE TAX REDUCTION STRATEGIES (Continued)

5. USE THE "NEWER" LIFE INSURANCE SERVICES TO SAVE

There are three types of life insurance you can use for investment purposes.

A. Single Premium Whole Life Insurance (SPWL)

SPWLs can be an excellent alternative to municipal bonds and CDs for savers who also want to add insurance values to their estate. They are life insurance policies bought with a single premium payment.

ADVANTAGES:

- The payment immediately becomes cash value in a policy.
- Policy pays tax-deferred interest.
- Principal and death benefits are guaranteed by the insurance company.
- Current interest rates are often competitive with CD rates.
- There are no initial sales charges.
- Death benefit income is tax free.

DISADVANTAGES:

- Cash value withdrawals or loans against cash values may be subject to income tax, and if you are under age 59½ they are subject to a 10 percent penalty.
- There may be early surrender penalties.

B. Variable Universal Life Insurance

Variable universal life insurance wraps mutual funds inside of an insurance contract. These policies can be single premium or can be paid annually. The tax consequences of any withdrawal will depend on how the policies are structured. Policies are sold by prospectus, which you must read carefully before investing.

ADVANTAGE:

- Should the mutual funds perform well, these policies can be a way of having tax-deferred accumulation and insurance death benefit for income protection in one investment.

DISADVANTAGE:

- Since some cash values can vary depending on the performance of the mutual funds you invest in, there are no guarantees of cash value accumulation. There are, however, guarantees of death benefit provided premiums are paid regularly.

"NEWER" LIFE INSURANCE (Continued)

C. Universal Life Insurance

Universal life insurance policies are newer forms of the old whole life, cash value policy. They offer more attractive investment returns and more flexibility than policies issued prior to their appearance. Policy costs include fees which cover taxes for the issuing carrier (about 2 percent of premium), a monthly adminstration charge ($5–$10 per month), and mortality expense. Commissions (fees) paid to the agent outside of the policy are generally lower than sales charges built into similar policies. Talk to your financial advisor about returns, guarantees, and costs.

ADVANTAGES

- These programs can be used as tax-favored accumulation investments as well as insurance policies.
- Cash value loans are not subject to income tax.
- Some universal life insurance policies are now no-load. No-load universal life policies have no sales or surrender charges so they may be more attractive investments than some conventional policies.

Notes on Life Insurance Policies

Costs, guarantees of principal and interest, investment performances, and tax consequences of different life insurance policies vary widely from company to company and program to program.

Some insurance investments are sold by prospectus which you should read carefully before investing.

Some life insurance policies allow cash value loans that are free from current income taxes. Consult a financial or insurance advisor before investing.

MY LIFE INSURANCE IS CURRENT

NINE TAX REDUCTION STRATEGIES (Continued)

6. USE ANNUITIES

Single-premium and variable-premium annuities can serve as high-yield, tax-deferred savings programs.

Fixed Annuities

Fixed annuities can provide guarantees of principal and fixed interest rates that are competitive with CDs and bonds but are tax deferred until money is withdrawn. Most fixed annuities have no sales charges and have surrender charges similar to CDs.

Variable Annuities

Variable annuities offer a way to defer capital gains and dividends earned on a wide variety of mutual funds. Principal or market value, the higher of the two, is usually guaranteed to the beneficiary at death of the annuitant.

Profits on all annuities are subject to income tax upon surrender or partial withdrawal. They are tax deferred, not tax free. However, after about 12 years of tax deferral, the tax-deferred compounding of dividends, interest, and capital gains may offset the taxes due. Surrendering or withdrawing money from an annuity before age 59½ carries a 10 percent tax penalty (like an IRA.) Some annuities purchased prior to August 1982 may have additional tax advantages—check with your advisors.

An annuity can be used inside or outside of a pension, IRA, or other retirement plan.

HOW TAX-DEFERRED ANNUITIES WORK

Issue date: Start deposits	Start income distributions	Termination date or death
X————————	————X————————	————X
Accumulation period: Interest and earnings accumulate, tax deferred	Distribution period: Interest and earnings taxed partially as income; and as partial return of principal	

NINE TAX REDUCTION STRATEGIES (Continued)

7. USE RENTAL REAL ESTATE

If your adjusted gross income, (AGI) is less than $100,000 a year, you may be eligible for $25,000 in real estate write-offs against income by owning and managing real estate. If you earn over $100,000 a year, you can carry rental real estate losses forward, using them to offset gains at the time of sale. If the depreciation, taxes, interest expenses, and maintenance costs come to more than rental income, they can still be used to reduce other forms of income. See your real estate, legal, and tax advisors on how to do this.

Illustration

Mary earns $60,000 a year and will pay a lot of tax unless she does something. She has $30,000 to invest in a tax shelter.

She consults with her advisors and decides to buy a $120,000 duplex with a $30,000 down payment.

Her rental income will be $1,000 a month. She will spend about $900 a month on the mortgage, taxes, insurance, and maintenance. She depreciates the property over 31 years.

Her rental income is $12,000 a year and her expenses, including depreciation, total $16,000 a year.

Mary can show a $4,000 loss on her tax return but she actually clears $1,200 tax free on the deal each year.

The write-off saves her $1,100 in taxes each year. (She's in the 28 percent tax bracket.)

If the property appreciates, she will have a nice profit several years down the road. She may be able to raise rents periodically to increase her net income.

Mary must manage this property herself and she must meet mortgage expenses whether or not her renters pay the rent.

NINE TAX REDUCTION STRATEGIES (Continued)

8. OWN AND OPERATE A FULL- OR PART-TIME BUSINESS

Most jobs in the United States are created by small businesses with fewer than 100 employees.

Congress gives all kinds of tax breaks to small business owners.

Many hobbies can be tied into satisfying and/or profitable part-time or full-time businesses. Expenses such as travel can be partially deductible as business expenses. But keep in mind that owning a business carries risks and liabilities that should not be taken lightly.

Retired professionals who become independent contractors may be able to offset taxable income with business expenses. The IRS carefully reviews these arrangements, so consult your tax advisor before you receive income.

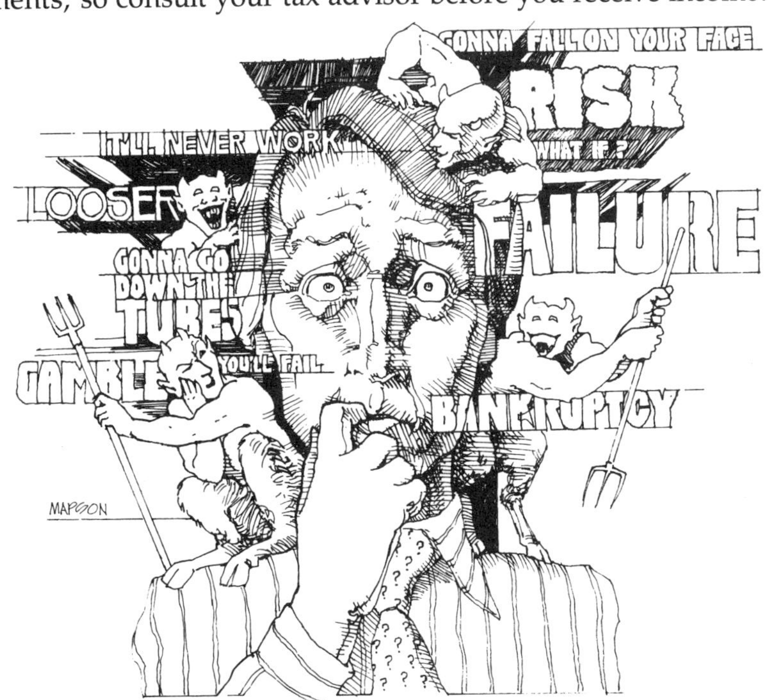

STARTING A NEW BUSINESS CAN BE SCARY... KNOW WHAT YOU ARE DOING*

*For an excellent book on this topic, order *STARTING YOUR NEW BUSINESS* using the form in the back of this book.

NINE TAX REDUCTION STRATEGIES (Continued)

9. USE TAX-FAVORED PARTNERSHIPS

There are three major types of tax-favored partnerships:

A. Historic Properties Partnerships

Following the federal guidelines to restore and preserve historic properties, investors are given tax credits that reduce the tax bill owed dollar for dollar. These partnerships may also produce income.

B. Low-Income Housing Partnerships

Beginning in 1988 and possibly extending beyond 1989, limited partnerships investing in low-income housing can receive a ten-year tax credit lowering their tax bill dollar for dollar. To qualify, your household income must be above $30,000 and below $200,000. These partnerships may produce income and capital gains in later years.

C. Oil and Gas Partnerships

The most speculative of the three classes of tax-favored programs, oil and gas partnerships offer depletion allowances and write-offs against *any* type of income if you enter as a general partner. These are income-producing partnerships. Write-offs as high as 50 percent in the first year are possible. Rules are complex, so see your financial and tax advisors before investing.

RECOMMENDATION

These limited partnerships offer significant tax reduction, but they are long-term investments. They usually require a minimum of $5,000, so you should only invest capital that you don't need for emergencies or opportunities. When used in conjunction with company savings plans, insurance programs, and tax-free bonds, they can reduce or eliminate income tax as well as taxes on retirement income, including tax on Social Security benefits and the catastrophic health care surtax.

SOME OTHER TAX-REDUCTION STRATEGIES TO CONSIDER

- Match passive income to passive losses.

- Consider charitable-giving strategies.

- Match capital gains to capital losses to reduce tax.

- Do not over or under contribute to withholding taxes.

TAX-REDUCTION SCENARIO

No Tax Planning vs Maximum Tax Planning
1. Single Worker

Income Items	No Plan	Max. Plan	Comments
Salary	$25,000	$25,000	
403B or 401K contribution	– 0	– 2,500	10% contribution (could be up to 25%)
W-2 Income	$25,000	$22,500	
Taxable interest on $40,000 savings @ 5%	+ 2,000	+ 500	Invest $30,000 in tax-deferred investments
	$27,000	$23,000	
Schedule E rents	– 0	– 2,000	Paper loss on $60,000 rental house
	$27,000	$21,000	
Schedule C business income or loss	– 0	– 1,000	Part-time business expenses or capital losses
	$27,000	$20,000	
IRA deductible contribution	– 0	– 2,000	Contribute $2,000 to IRA
Adjusted gross income	$27,000	$18,000	
Personal deductions	– 2,000	– 4,000	Refinance loans on house to pay off credit cards ($20K–40K)
	$25,000	$14,000	
Personal exemption	– 2,000	– 2,000	
Net taxable income	$23,000	$12,000	
1989 tax	4,029	1,800	
Tax credits	0	– 750	Invest $5,000 in limited tax partnership: 15% tax credit
Final tax	$ 4,029	$ 1,050	
Tax payments	3,600	2,000	Reduce withholding to invest or spend $1,600
Tax due (–) or refund (+)	– $429	+ $950	

TAX-REDUCTION SCENARIO (Continued)

No Tax Planning vs Maximum Tax Planning
2. Married Couple

Income Items	No Plan	Max. Plan	Comments
Combined salaries	$50,000	$50,000	
403B or 401K contribution	– 0	– 5,000	10% contribution (could be up to 25% but no more than $7,627 in 1989 (per person)
W-2 Income	$50,000	$45,000	
Taxable interest on $40,000 savings @ 5%	+ 2,000	+ 500	Invest $30,000 in tax-deferred investments
	$52,000	$45,500	
Schedule E rents	– 0	– 2,000	Paper loss on $60,000 rental house
	$52,000	$43,500	
Schedule C business income or loss	– 0	– 1,000	Part-time business expenses or capital losses
	$52,000	$42,500	
IRA deductible contribution	– 0	– 3,000	Contribute $1,500 per employed person to IRA
Adjusted gross income	$52,000	$39,500	
Personal deductions	– 4,000	– 8,000	Refinance loans on house to pay off credit cards ($20K–40K)
	$48,000	$31,500	
Personal exemption	– 4,000	– 4,000	
Net taxable income	$44,000	$27,500	
1989 tax	8,296	4,125	
Tax credits	0	– 750	Invest $5,000 in limited tax partnership: 15% tax credit
Final tax	$ 8,296	$ 3,375	
Tax payments	7,800	4,000	Reduce withholding to invest or spend $3,800
Tax due (–) or refund (+)	– $496	+ $625	

CONCLUSION

YOU CAN WIN THE TAX-REDUCTION GAME

- Careful planning and record keeping are essential.
- Using financial advisors should save more in taxes than you pay in fees.
- Plan tax strategies before the tax year ends to get the most tax savings.
- Putting money away into tax-qualified plans is one of the main ways to reduce taxes and build wealth.
- Despite the changes in the tax laws, there are still a lot of legal ways to reduce income taxes.

PART V

Planning for Retirement

> *"A successful retirement begins with a positive attitude."*
>
> E. N. Chapman

TRANSITIONS

INTRODUCTION

The purpose of retirement planning is to achieve financial independence. You need to build and then maintain a retirement income that will satisfy your lifestyle. The transition to retirement involves repositioning assets, benefits, and lifestyle which requires careful planning.

OBJECTIVES

Once you have determined the lifestyle you desire, you will need to meet certain objectives with your resources. You should commit to the following:

1. Your assets and benefits shall generate a steady, predictable income.
2. Your assets shall grow enough to keep pace with inflation after taxes.
3. Your assets and benefits shall be protected from risks and losses due to market cycles, poor management, ill health, or death.

You can learn to invest with:

- Low risk
- Low tax
- Low cost

TIME TO RETIRE!

EXPECTATIONS

Your income planning will be affected by certain assumptions and expectations.

1. HOW LONG WILL YOU LIVE?

   Perhaps longer than you think—so your resources must last a long time. Your financial plans must meet the life-stage needs of early, middle, and late retirement years. In the event of the death of one spouse, you need to understand how the survivor will receive and manage income.

2. WHAT WILL BE THE EFFECT OF INFLATION NOW AND IN FUTURE YEARS?

   Even a modest rate of 5 percent inflation will double your cost of living in fourteen years. Your income must be adjusted for inflation to protect your lifestyle.

3. WHAT WILL THE ECONOMY DO OVER THE YEARS?

   No single pattern of income will work for all situations. You will need to review your financial plans periodically. You should utilize an asset management strategy to adjust to cycles of inflation and deflation, boom and bust, low taxes or high taxes.

4. HOW MUCH RISK ARE YOU WILLING TO INCUR TO MINIMIZE THE IMPACT OF A CHANGING ECONOMY?

   You will face an interest-rate risk, a default risk, a market risk, and an inflation risk. Your financial plan should not expose your assets to any more risks than are necessary to achieve your retirement goals.

5. WHAT KINDS OF DEMAND WILL YOUR FAMILY PLACE UPON YOUR RESOURCES?

   Retirees in the family are sometimes seen as ''deep pockets'' or ''family bankers.'' How will you deal with this?

MANAGING YOUR PLAN

Review your plan periodically. You should be sure that assets are diversified to reduce risk and increase returns. You will also need to adjust your plan to changes in your circumstances, the economy, or the marketplace. Tax preparation is an excellent time to review your financial and retirement plans.

CHECKLIST AHEAD

RETIREMENT READINESS APPRAISAL

Answer yes or no to the following:

_______ Have you clearly defined your retirement goals and objectives?

_______ Have you developed a clear idea of the lifestyle you want to have and discussed this with your family?

_______ Have you reviewed your current employee and government benefit programs and resources?

_______ Have you compiled a detailed asset and liability summary, including estimates of current yields and relationship to inflation?

_______ Have you obtained a clear understanding of all your sources of income and expenditure, including the tax consequences?

_______ Have you performed an in-depth analysis of all your portfolio holdings, including real estate, savings, and tangibles?

_______ Have you prepared a current budget and outlined a future retirement budget?

_______ Have you reviewed and updated all your pertinent legal documents, such as wills, trusts and beneficiary designations?

_______ Have you reviewed all your insurance programs to make sure you are adequately protected?

_______ Have you established an organized record-keeping and document safekeeping system that is updated regularly?

_______ Have you built a team of advisors you can use to help achieve and maintain your financial independence?

If you answered yes to 9 or more questions, then you are in a good position to retire successfully.

If you answered yes to 5–8 questions, then you are getting ready, but you have some work yet to do.

If you answered no, or you are not sure about most of the questions, then you are not ready for retirement and you have a lot of learning, organizing, and thinking to do yet to get ready.

RECOMMENDATION

Take a retirement training class or books such as *Personal Financial Fitness* or *Comfort Zones,* both of which are available from Crisp Publications, Inc., 95 First St., Los Altos, California 94022.

THE THREE RETIREMENT PLANNING STAGES

You can never start too early to plan for financial independence. Early planning can maximize your savings and investment returns over the years. But—if time has slipped by or if other family concerns such as raising or educating the children have delayed your planning—late planning is better than no planning. Depending on your age and employment status, your planning will fall into one of the following categories: *preretirement planning,* which takes place from age 40 onward, *retirement transition planning,* which takes place in the first six months during the year in which you retire, and *postretirement planning,* which lasts for many years after retirement.

1. Preretirement Planning

In this phase you are most concerned about:

- Setting goals and deciding on lifestyle alternatives beginning no later than age 40.
- Identifying and learning about funding methods and techniques.
- Developing and using techniques for accumulating assets.
- Using methods for reducing income taxes and costs.
- Managing your response to economic and social variables such as inflation, the economy, the financial markets, your family circumstances.
- Review all sources of income and investment, wills and other pertinent documents, family asset titles, all benefits programs from prior employment.

2. Retirement Transition Planning

In this phase you are most concerned about:

- Refining and restructuring retirement lifestyle goals to be as realistic as possible.
- Repositioning assets and benefits to begin to generate a steady retirement income.
- Analyzing funding methods to fund your new retirement lifestyle, and adjusting income and expenditures to sustain your lifestyle.
- Identifying pension, deferred compensation, and IRA distribution alternatives that will produce steady income, incur low taxes, and save money.
- Building a team of advisors to help you implement your retirement lifestyle. You will need an accountant to review tax calculations in your plan, an attorney to review your estate plans, and a financial planner to coordinate the team you have assembled to construct and manage your retirement income portfolio.

THE THREE RETIREMENT PLANNING STAGES (Continued)

3. Postretirement Planning

In this phase you are most concerned about:

- Refining goals and objectives so they can be realistic in satisfying your lifestyle needs and desires.
- Maximizing your income from all funding sources while being careful to protect your assets from risk, inflation, taxes, and unnecessary costs.
- Organizing assets to produce and maintain a safe, steady income with as little complexity as possible.
- Estate planning so all assets can be immediately transferred to beneficiaries at low cost in the event of disability or death.
- Enjoying major purchases, pleasures, hobbies, trips, and luxuries, which you deserve for having planned successfully.
- Enriching yourself and others through community service, social activity, continuing education, and volunteer work such as fund raising.

SOLVING THE EARLY RETIREMENT DILEMMA

The good news is—you can retire before age 59½ if you want. The bad news is—you may experience tax penalties and benefit reductions if you retire early. The next four pages provide four solutions to the early retirement dilemma:

SOLUTION #1
Annuitize Benefits

The answer is simple—annuitize your IRA and 401K! The IRS will allow you to make level monthly, quarterly, semiannual, or annual withdrawals from tax-savings plans if done properly.

First, combine the money in your 401K and IRA. You may want to roll the taxable portion of a 401K into a self-directed IRA. Place all separate IRAs accumulated over the years into one self-directed IRA. Now subtract your current age from your average life expectancy.

Example:	Life expectancy age	81
	Current age	– 55
		26 years

Divide the 26 into the total dollars in your self-directed IRA.

Example:	401K	$70,000
	IRA	21,000
	Total	$91,000 divided by 26 = $3,500

You can now have approximately $300 more income per month to age 81! This can help supplement early retirement income until Social Security kicks in at age 62. Meanwhile, the $91,000 may be earning more income than you are withdrawing, so it continues to grow in value until you are past any penalties for early withdrawals. After 5 years you could change your withdrawals to higher amounts and stop the lower annuity payment.

A word of caution: To annuitize tax-qualified savings plans like IRAs and 401Ks, you must follow an IRS-approved formula. If you alter your withdrawal at any time during the first five years or before age 59½, you are subject to the 10 percent penalty starting with the first withdrawal you made.

Summarize your calculations in a letter to the IRS and submit it with your tax return. As always, consult your tax advisor to be sure you have done this properly, particularly your actuarial calculation.

SOLUTION #2
Pay the Penalties and Invest For High Income

Roll your 401Ks and IRAs into a self-directed IRA that allows you to have a variety of investments in one IRA and build a high-yield portfolio that pays you a high income until Social Security begins.

Example:	401K	70,000	Earning 8% =	$5,600
	IRAs	21,000	Earning 7% =	$1,400
		91,000	7.7%	$7,000

Roll all to one self-directed IRA worth 91,000 *TO EARN:*

$20,000 in High-Yield Money Market at 7%	$1,400
$20,000 in Long-Term CDs at 9%	1,800
$30,000 in High-Yield Bonds at 11%	3,300
$21,000 in Quality Stocks earning 14%	2,940
$91,000	$9,440

Draw $8,000	per year from Money Market at $666 per month
– 800	10% annual tax penalty for early withdrawal
$7,200	divided by 12 = $600 per month or $300 a month more than annuitization per year.

Meanwhile, the IRA is growing at $1,440 a year in value. Your high-income and growth portfolio is earning more than the penalty and paying twice as much a month in income as the annuitization strategy.

A word of caution:
There are stock and bond market risks associated with this strategy as well as interest-rate fluctuation associated with CDs and Money Market Funds. There may also be commission costs included in setting up the IRA investments. Consult your investment advisor.

SOLUTION #3
Use an Immediate Short-Term Annuity

If you are over age 59½, consider 10-year averaging on the 401K and use about one-third of the money to buy an immediate annuity income for 5 years or until Social Security starts. Leave the IRA untouched and invest the remaining after-tax 401K balance in high-yield, tax-free bonds or in tax-deferred annuities.

Example:	401K	$70,000
	IRA	$21,000
		$91,000

Take $70,000 out of the 401K and if you are over age 50 on January 1, 1986, pay a one-time 10-year forward-averaging tax of approximately $9,000.

Leave the IRA alone earning 8% for 5 years.

$70,000
– 9,000 tax
$61,000
–$25,000 invested in 5-year Immediate Annuity guaranteeing income of $19 per month per $1,000 = $475 per month for 60 months × 12 = $5,700 per year. Only 16%, or $850 of this $5,700 income is taxable. In 5 years, all the $25,000 plus interest has been paid to you.

–$36,000 invested in a Tax-Deferred Annuity earning 8%. In 5 years your account is worth

$70,000
+$32,000 IRA value
$102,000

You have received monthly income with no tax penalties and a special one-time tax.

A word of caution:
If you are under age 59½ and use this strategy, it will not work as well because you will pay a 10 percent tax penalty for early withdrawal from your plan.

SOLUTION #4
Live on Nonqualified Assets Until Age 59½

If you have assets outside of your retirement plans, such as savings, stocks, real estate proceeds, etc., use these assets to live on until you are past penalties on your retirement plans. Roll your 401K and IRAs into one IRA and let it grow tax-deferred until you need it or until you are past age 59½.

Example:	401K	$70,000	
	IRA	21,000	
	Savings	20,000	
	Stocks	20,000	
	Real Estate Proceeds	50,000	from sale or loan
		$181,000	

Combine 401K and IRAs and let it grow tax deferred until you are over 59½ years old.

Invest your stock and real estate proceeds of $70,000 in a high yielding mutual fund and draw 12% a year (or $8,400) out of the fund. Using a monthly systematic withdrawal program, this will pay you $700 each month. When you pass age 59½ begin to draw money from your IRA and reduce your systematic withdrawal program to 6% to rebuild the value of your mutual fund. You may be consuming principal in your fund before age 59½, but you are paying no tax penalties for early withdrawal and you have a steady monthly income from your fund. See your investment advisor on how mutual funds work and remember to read the prospectus before investing.

SOLVING THE LATE RETIREMENT DILEMMA

Employees who work beyond normal retirement age 65 may face a different dilemma.

If you choose to continue tax deferral in a pension plan, 401K, or IRA you may have to make large mandatory withdrawals by age 70½, which could trigger a tax on Social Security. If the annual modified adjusted Social Security calculation exceeds $32,000 married filing jointly, or $25,000 if filing single, a portion of your Social Security may be taxed.

You will also have to pay the Medicare catastrophic health care surtax if over age 65.

RECOMMENDATIONS

- Try to keep taxable income as low as possible by moving investments to tax-free and tax-deferred positions.
- You may want to consider refinancing your home to offset income, however this will not count towards reducing the possible tax on Social Security.
- Make the maximum IRA "tax-deductible" contribution.
- Make the maximum contribution to your company tax-deferred savings plan.
- Consider the use of federal tax credit programs.
- Construct a charitable-giving program.
- If you or your spouse have your own business, or own rental property, the Social Security tax calculation and annual income taxes may be reduced.
- If you do work beyond age 70½, you may earn any amount of income without your Social Security payment being reduced.

ESTIMATING RETIREMENT INCOME AND EXPENSES

To plan your retirement income effectively, you need to decide what you want your lifestyle to be. Use the form below to estimate how much this will cost monthly and annually. When you match your income with your expenses, you will find the areas where adjustments need to be made. The match you construct between what you want to spend and what you have to spend is the financial reality of your lifestyle.

Expense Item	**Realistic Monthly**	**Realistic Annual**
Housing	$	$
Utilities		
Food		
Dining out		
Taxes		
Insurance		
Medical		
Travel		
Recreation		
Credit costs		
Donations		
Clothing		
Savings/Investing		
Misc. Personal		
Gifts		
Other		
Other		
Total Expenses	$	$

INCOME ANALYSIS WORKSHEET:

Investment Assets

To analyze your income sources, use the following worksheet. Use approximate numbers and identify annual taxable or tax-free income. Identify whether or not you are spending or reinvesting some of the income. Break it down on a monthly basis.

(1) **Source of Income**	(2) **Value of* Principal**	(3) **Percent* Yield**	(4) **Taxable* Annual Income**	(5) **Tax-Free* Annual Income**	(6) **Monthly* Income**	(7) **Spend or Reinvest**
Total income from all sources						

*(2) × (3) = (4) or (5) /12 = (6)

Financial Planning Ideas to Consider

1. Compare your monthly expense budget with your income analysis. Do you have enough income to cover expenses?

2. If not, how could you generate more income? Could you get higher yields than you are now presently receiving? Are there assets that are not generating income that could be repositioned to produce income? Could you reduce the income taxes you pay by moving taxable income assets to produce tax-free income?

3. Are you receiving your income monthly or do you have to wait months for it? Try to set up your assets for monthly income.

4. If you have more than enough current income, could you be reinvesting gains to offset future inflation? Are all your income assets indexed to inflation?

TO GO OR NOT TO GO—EARLY RETIREMENT?

Many companies now offer early retirement incentives to employees for a variety of reasons. Receiving an offer is often both an exciting and threatening experience loaded with emotional and financial opportunities and risks.

Before you accept an offer to retire early, answer these questions:

1. Do I want to leave this job now?
2. Do I want to pursue a different job now?
3. Do I want to stop working completely now?
4. Do I want to do this same job, but at another company?
5. Will I have enough income and benefits with this offer to maintain or improve my current lifestyle?
6. Will my family benefit if I accept this offer now?

If you can answer yes to most or all of these questions, then taking the offer will probably be a satisfying choice. If you answer no to most or all of these questions, then it may be better to stay.

Is It Enough? How do I know if it is financially enough to maintain or improve my lifestyle?

Use the income information from the offer with the previous worksheets, ''Retirement Readiness Appraisal,'' ''Estimating Expenses,'' and ''Income Analysis.''

The real issue to decide, however, is not whether or not you have enough money, but ''Do I really want to quit this job now?'' Even if you have enough to live on from the offer and your current net worth, you may not feel good about giving up your work now.

If, on the other hand, you can't wait to leave, but the offer is not enough, you need to look at ways to restructure your income, net worth, and lifestyle to maintain or improve your quality of life.

Other Issues To Consider What will you lose in the future by leaving now? How disrupted will your family life be if you go now?

RECOMMENDATION

When you receive the details of the offer, take a little time off to talk with your family and advisors about the offer and about what you want to do with your life and resources. These offers can often force us to consider how we really want to live our lives. An early retirement offer can often open a door to a whole new lifestyle.

PART VI

Retirement Income

DON'T POSTPONE RETIREMENT PLANNING

ESTATE PLANNING WITH YOUR BENEFITS

Your gross estate is the value of all of your assets plus all life insurance and employee benefits at your demise.

The total value of your estate can be expanded significantly by using employee benefits such as:

- Basic and supplemental life insurance benefits that often equal two to six times your annual salary.
- Pension benefits for you and your beneficiaries.
- Savings plans which belong to you and your beneficiaries.
- Stock purchase plans that belong to you and your beneficiaries.
- Credit union savings plans that provide benefits to you and your beneficiaries.
- Social Security income and survivor benefits.

It is not difficult to build an estate for you and your survivors worth several hundreds of thousands of dollars or more by participating in these benefit programs. Employee benefits can be distributed to beneficiaries outside of the probate process.

RECOMMENDATIONS

Keep your beneficiary designations up to date on all your benefits. You need to update your beneficiary designations when:

- You marry or divorce.
- You have children.
- One of your beneficiaries dies.
- You wish to change beneficiary sharing arrangements.
- You set up trusts or new wills.

You need to consult an attorney before making any major changes in your wishes concerning your beneficiaries.

When your total estate assets exceed $600,000, you may wish to consult an attorney concerning the advantages of using trusts and gifting programs to avoid or reduce possible federal and state estate and inheritance taxes.

SETTING A RETIREMENT DATE

Before you actually retire, consult your advisors and your benefits personnel about the best time to leave.

Sometimes, just a small difference in time can mean a big difference in taxes, benefits, or costs.

RECOMMENDATION

After consulting your advisors, set your retirement date early into the new calendar year, so you get a full year of service credit for Social Security, pension, vacation time, etc. Probably the best time to retire is in February or March, so you have most of that year to plan the tax consequences of your benefits.

AVOID TRANSFER TRAUMA

When transferring benefits from one plan to another, avoid transferring the tax-free portions of tax-qualified retirement plans and pensions into a new tax-deferred plan. This will cause money that could have remained tax free in your hands to be subject to taxation when you withdraw it from the new plan.

EXAMPLE

Harry retired after 25 years with his present employer. He took another job and decided to transfer his pension lump sum and profit-sharing plan into his new company's 401K and leave it there for a few years. He did not consult his advisors and found out later from his accountant that $20,000 of that pension and $10,000 in his older profit-sharing plan could have been taken out of the plans without any tax. Now those funds are invested in a new tax-deferred plan and any withdrawals will be taxable.

PENSION OPTIONS

Overview

There are four main sources of income in retirement:

- Personal investment income in which you control the assets and the tax consequences.
- Social Security income which provides a monthly benefit that you do not control, and which may or may not be partially taxable depending on how your assets and income are structured.
- Employee pensions that are usually monthly annuity income programs which you do not control and are usually fully taxable.
- Personal retirement plan savings, which you may control the tax consequences to a large extent.

PENSION OPTIONS (Continued)

There are a variety of ways to draw money from pensions.

Lump-Sum Distributions

Many companies no longer offer a lump-sum option. If the company does, there are several factors to consider.

1. You may choose to leave the lump sum in your pension plan until age 70½.

   If you do not need immediate income from your pension, or you plan to begin a second career, this may be a good option. But you may want to consider these factors before electing to leave the lump sum with your company:

   - How attractive are the yields inside the plan? Defined benefit plans have no stated yield. How flexible is the plan to allow for asset reallocation in a timely fashion? You may be able to find better results and more flexibility outside the plan.

   - If emergency money is needed, how quickly can money be removed and how often?

   - When you reach age 70½ the lump sum can be significant in size. You will have to withdraw actuarially calculated sums every year. This could produce severe tax consequences which could cause Social Security to become taxable, move you into a higher tax bracket as well as trigger the Medicare Catastrophic Health Care surtax! The distribution at age 70½ is unavoidable under current tax law.

   - There may be a nontaxable portion in your pension program—you may want to immediately remove this portion at retirement because many plans have a ''trust-to-trust'' transfer. Once the transfer occurs, you cannot remove the nontaxable portion. Therefore, it is imperative to remove it before the transfer takes place. Have your company benefits counselor calculate the nontaxable portion.

PENSION OPTIONS (Continued)

2. You could roll qualified plan money into a self-directed IRA.

Here you can have fast access, control investments, have unlimited flexibility, and possibly outperform the returns you would have received by leaving the benefit with your company. Again, be certain that nontaxable pension dollars are withdrawn prior to transfer.

Here too, at age 70½ you must begin making withdrawals and if planning is not done, considerable taxes could result.

3. You may elect to use the five- or ten-year forward-average tax calculation.

The ten-year average option is available if you were 50 on or before January 1, 1986. You must pay a 10 percent penalty in addition if you are not over age 59½ when the withdrawal is made.

This option should produce a lower tax than your current annual rate. Have a professional tax consultant or financial planner review the tax liability for each calculation before you make the decision. Often when this option is chosen, the money is invested in tax-advantaged programs producing current income and growth.

RECOMMENDATION

Tax-qualified savings plans such as 401Ks can sometimes be rolled into company pension programs. If income is not needed from this source at retirement, it can grow, tax deferred. Remember, only the taxable portion can be retained in the company plan in most cases.

If you are over age 59½, a better strategy would be to utilize 10-year forward averaging (if your 50th birthday was on or before 01/01/86). When 401K amounts are under $100,000 taxable distributions, the 10-year forward tax rate is usually more attractive than the 5-year averaging. Consult your tax professional or financial planner for advice and calculation of the tax rate.

PENSION ANNUITY DISTRIBUTIONS AND PENSION MAXIMIZATION

Life annuity and survivorship annuity options both guarantee specific monthly payments for as long as you or your spouse live.

A life annuity offers a higher monthly payment than a survivorship annuity while the employee is alive. However, at death a spouse will receive nothing.

A survivorship annuity option usually reduces the single annuity monthly payment by 10 to 25 percent while the employee is alive. At the death of the employee, the surviving spouse will receive 50 percent of the payment received while the employee was alive. Some insurance carriers now require married couples to elect survivorship if they want to continue receiving free medical coverage in retirement.

These annuities rarely have an automatic annual cost of living adjustment. Widow(er)s who are dependent on the survivor annuity benefit endure financial hardship, particularly if they enjoy long, healthy lives many years after their employee-spouse has died.

Some company retirement annuities do not allow a retired employee to change their election once they start receiving monthly payments. So, if an employee chooses a survivorship annuity and their spouse predeceases them, they cannot change to the higher paying life annuity. Consult your benefits manual.

Some retirement annuities guarantee payments to heirs for life or a certain period of five, ten, or fifteen years after the death of the employee. The employee gets the annuity for life. If he or she dies before the end of the agreed period, the spouse gets the guaranteed payments until the end of five, ten, or fifteen years. If the spouse dies within the agreed period, the heirs get the guaranteed payments.

THE WIDOW'S DILEMMA

Bill is age 62 and Mary age 60. Bill wants to retire now and has a pension election to make. Mary has no pension. Bill's pension options look like this:

Pension Option	Monthly Income		Assets for Income	
	To Bill	To Mary	To Bill	To Mary
Life annuity	$2,000	$ 0	$ 0	$ 0
50% survivorship annuity	1,800	900	0	0
25% survivorship annuity	1,900	375	0	0
Life and 15 years certain	1,542	1,542*	0	0

*If Bill dies before 15 years pass

Which option should they choose?

Read on!

THE SOLUTION: PENSION MAXIMIZATION WITH LIFE INSURANCE

If Bill elected the life annuity for the highest monthly income while he were alive, how would Mary be provided for?

There are two possibilities:

1. Sufficient income from other investments and assets outside the plan.

2. Life insurance. Bill would need to target the death benefit so that monthly withdrawals of principal and interest would provide Mary with 80 percent of the life annuity benefit—$1,600 per month.

The life insurance contract should be at the lowest possible cost and be a whole life policy. Premium should be paid if possible by using after-tax distribution from the 401K plan. Use ten-year averaging, if applicable, for the taxable portion. The policy should be paid up as soon as possible. It is important that the policy comply with current tax law so that policy loans are nontaxable.

A quality policy should perform at net average money market rates (near 6 percent) after all expense charges, commissions, and mortality costs are deducted.

This takes careful shopping and planning, but may be worth it.

BILL AND MARY'S PENSION MAXIMIZATION

By integrating his pension election with life insurance, Bill gets the following benefits:

- Bill and Mary have the most monthly income available during Bill's lifetime.
- Upon Bill's death, Mary will receive the death benefit from Bill's insurance policy, *income tax free.* It can then be placed in a tax-favored investment, assuring Mary 80 percent of the life annuity income they had while Bill was alive. This is substantially higher than the 25 or 50 percent offered by survivorship.
- If Mary predeceases Bill, Bill could make tax-free withdrawals of principal and interest to supplement his income; cancel the policy (if there are no surrender penalties) and invest the premiums paid plus interest. Or he could borrow against the policy—in most cases up to 90 percent—leaving the remaining death benefit for his children.
- If both die in a common disaster, a pension annuity would not, in most cases, be payable to their heirs. But the death benefit of a life insurance policy would pass free of income tax to heirs. For pension programs with no lump-sum distribution option, this is a way to produce a lump sum for an estate, protect a spouse, and receive the highest monthly income during the employee's lifetime. This can be accomplished with minimal risk, minimal cost, and minimal tax.

RECOMMENDATION

There are a few important things to remember if using pension maximization.

- The employee must predetermine if he or she can be insured with a standard rating. A trial application should be submitted and approved by the insurance company. This should be done before electing the life annuity option and before the spouse signs away his or her right to a survivorship interest.
- Prepay full premiums if possible. If not, make sure that there are adequate resources to make premium payments as long as necessary. In this case the policy should have an automatic premium payment feature should a payment be missed.
- Remember that death benefit minus any loans should always be sufficient to provide the employee's spouse with adequate income.
- Review beneficiary and secondary beneficiary designations regularly.
- Shop carefully for insurance with lowest cost, highest guarantees, and best yield.

PENSION MAXIMIZATION WORKSHEET

1. Current age Employee ______ Spouse ______	2. Age of planned retirement: ______
3. Retirement you will receive: Single annuity, $ ______ per month Joint and survivor annuity, $ ______ per month	
4. Total death benefit of all cash-value life insurance in force: $ ______	
5. Total value of current investments, excluding personal property and primary residence:* Liquid investments $ ______ Rental property, raw land, etc. $ ______	
6. Value of savings plan: $ ______	

How Much Insurance?

First, calculate 80 percent of the employee's life annuity. This assumes that most major costs are fixed and costs will not be much less for the employee's widow than while the employee was alive.

Then you need to know how much insurance death benefit is needed to provide monthly payments of this amount.

You also need to know the spouse's age. The younger the spouse, the longer the potential income stream needs to continue.

Let's look at an example using the table on page 96. Assume the employee's life annuity was $2,000 per month. Assume we could find a reasonably safe investment that would yield 8 percent. The employee's spouse is 62 years old. Her expected life span is another 20 years. Find on the table, under "Years Remaining in Term," 20 years. Now look down that column until you find a number close to $1,600. We find $1,672.88. To the left, find the column in bold print, "Amount." The insurance benefit required is $200,000, which at 8 percent withdrawing principal and interest will produce $1,672.88 per month for the surviving spouse for twenty years.

Obviously, you can use different variables depending on your other assets, income, Social Security, age, and the rate of return you choose.

---

* We exclude personal effects and primary residence from our asset calculations because surviving spouses least need to disrupt their living space and personal effects after the death of loved ones.

8% Monthly Payments

Necessary to Amortize a Loan

AMOUNT	25	24	23	22	21	20	15	10	5
	YEARS REMAINING IN TERM								
100	0.77	0.78	0.79	0.81	0.82	0.84	0.96	1.21	2.03
200	1.54	1.56	1.59	1.61	1.64	1.67	1.91	2.43	4.06
300	2.32	2.35	2.38	2.42	2.46	2.51	2.87	3.64	6.08
400	3.09	3.13	3.17	3.22	3.28	3.35	3.82	4.85	8.11
500	3.86	3.91	3.97	4.03	4.10	4.18	4.78	6.07	10.14
600	4.63	4.69	4.76	4.84	4.92	5.02	5.73	7.28	12.17
700	5.40	5.47	5.55	5.64	5.74	5.86	6.69	8.49	14.19
800	6.17	6.26	6.35	6.45	6.56	6.69	7.65	9.71	16.22
900	6.95	7.04	7.14	7.26	7.38	7.53	8.60	10.92	18.25
1,000	7.72	7.82	7.93	8.06	8.20	8.36	9.56	12.13	20.28
2,000	15.44	15.64	15.87	16.12	16.41	16.73	19.11	24.27	40.55
3,000	23.15	23.46	23.80	24.19	24.61	25.09	28.67	36.40	60.83
4,000	30.87	31.28	31.74	32.25	32.82	33.46	38.23	48.53	81.11
5,000	38.59	39.10	39.67	40.31	41.02	41.82	47.78	60.66	101.38
6,000	46.31	46.92	47.61	48.37	49.23	50.19	57.34	72.80	121.66
7,000	54.03	54.74	55.54	56.43	57.43	58.55	66.90	84.93	141.93
8,000	61.75	62.56	63.48	64.49	65.63	66.92	76.45	97.06	162.21
9,000	69.46	70.38	71.41	72.56	73.84	75.28	86.01	109.19	182.49
10,000	77.18	78.21	79.35	80.62	82.04	83.64	95.57	121.33	202.76
15,000	116.77	117.31	119.02	120.93	123.06	125.47	143.35	181.99	304.15
20,000	154.36	156.41	158.69	161.24	164.09	167.29	191.13	242.66	405.53
25,000	192.95	195.51	198.36	201.54	205.11	209.11	238.91	303.32	506.91
30,000	231.54	234.62	238.04	241.85	246.13	250.93	286.70	363.98	608.29
35,000	270.14	273.72	277.71	282.16	287.15	292.75	334.48	424.65	709.67
40,000	308.73	312.82	317.38	322.47	328.17	334.58	382.26	485.31	811.06
45,000	347.32	351.92	357.05	362.78	369.19	376.40	430.04	545.97	912.44
50,000	385.91	391.03	396.73	403.09	410.21	418.22	477.83	606.64	1013.82
55,000	424.50	430.13	436.40	443.40	451.24	460.04	525.61	667.30	1115.20
60,000	463.09	469.23	476.07	483.71	492.26	501.86	573.39	727.97	1216.58
65,000	501.68	508.34	515.74	524.02	533.28	543.69	621.17	788.63	1317.97
70,000	540.27	547.44	555.42	564.32	574.30	585.51	668.96	849.29	1419.35
71,000	547.99	555.26	563.35	572.39	582.50	593.87	678.51	861.43	1439.62
72,000	555.71	563.08	571.29	580.45	590.71	602.24	688.07	873.56	1459.90
73,000	563.43	570.90	579.22	588.51	598.91	610.60	697.63	885.69	1480.18
74,000	571.14	578.72	587.15	596.57	607.12	618.97	707.18	897.82	1500.45
75,000	578.86	586.54	595.09	604.63	615.32	627.33	716.74	909.96	1520.73
76,000	586.58	594.36	603.02	612.70	623.53	635.69	726.30	922.09	1541.01
77,000	594.30	602.18	610.96	620.76	631.73	644.06	735.85	934.22	1561.28
78,000	602.02	610.00	618.89	628.82	639.93	652.42	745.41	946.36	1581.56
79,000	609.73	617.82	626.83	636.88	648.14	660.79	754.96	958.49	1601.83
80,000	617.45	625.64	634.76	644.94	656.34	669.15	764.52	970.52	1622.11
81,000	625.17	633.46	642.70	653.00	664.55	677.52	774.08	982.75	1642.39
82,000	632.89	641.28	650.63	661.07	672.75	685.88	783.63	994.89	1662.66
83,000	640.61	649.10	658.57	669.13	680.96	694.25	793.19	1007.02	1682.94
84,000	648.33	656.93	666.50	677.19	689.19	702.61	802.75	1019.15	1703.22
85,000	656.04	664.75	674.43	685.25	697.36	710.97	812.30	1031.28	1723.49
86,000	663.76	672.57	682.37	693.31	705.57	719.34	821.86	1043.42	1743.77
87,000	671.48	680.39	690.30	701.37	713.77	727.70	831.42	1055.55	1764.05
88,000	679.20	688.21	698.24	709.44	721.98	736.07	840.97	1067.68	1784.32
89,000	686.92	696.03	706.17	717.50	730.18	744.43	850.53	1079.82	1804.60
90,000	694.63	703.85	714.11	725.56	738.39	752.80	860.09	1091.95	1824.87
100,000	771.82	782.05	793.45	806.18	820.43	836.44	955.65	1213.28	2027.64
110,000	849.00	860.26	872.80	886.80	902.47	920.08	1051.22	1334.60	2230.40
120,000	926.18	938.46	952.14	967.41	984.51	1003.73	1146.78	1455.93	2433.17
130,000	1003.36	1016.67	1031.49	1048.03	1066.56	1087.37	1242.35	1577.26	2635.93
140,000	1080.54	1094.88	1110.83	1128.65	1148.60	1171.02	1337.91	1698.59	2838.69
150,000	1157.72	1173.08	1190.18	1209.27	1230.64	1254.66	1433.48	1819.91	3041.46
200,000	1543.63	1564.11	1586.90	1612.36	1640.86	1672.88	1911.30	2426.55	4055.28
250,000	1929.54	1955.14	1983.63	2015.44	2051.07	2091.10	2389.13	3033.19	5069.10
300,000	2315.45	2346.16	2380.36	2418.53	2461.28	2509.32	2866.96	3639.83	6082.92

STRATEGIES TO IMPROVE YOUR BOTTOM LINE AFTER RETIREMENT

Reduce Unnecessary Costs

There are several things you can do to reduce monthly expenses during retirement:

- Pay off the mortgage on the house if you plan to live there for many years and don't need the tax deductions.
- Buy cars and major appliances with cash from investments, rather than financing these purchases.
- Cash in your life insurance policies that are no longer needed if you have adequate income and assets.
- Plan major purchases carefully so that you get the best prices and don't have to finance purchases with high-cost credit. Consider using home equity loans.
- Eliminate expenses attached to the job, such as the expenses of a second car, commuting costs, work clothing costs, lunches.

Reposition Underutilized Assets

If you want more income during retirement, look at ways to generate income from underutilized and nonliquid assets:

- Sell real estate that you do not use and reinvest the proceeds.
- Take cash values of older insurance policies you feel you do not need and reinvest the money.
- Sell tangible assets such as collectibles and artifacts to which you are not attached.
- Sell growth assets such as low-yield stocks or mutual funds and invest in higher-yield assets with greater stability of principal.

BUILD A HIGH-YIELD PORTFOLIO

While safety of principal is a major concern, many people should significantly increase their income by building a diversified high-yield portfolio of investments. You need to consult with your investment advisors about this strategy because it involves some risks that must be understood and accepted before putting it into action.

EXAMPLE

Rick and Tami have investments and savings of $100,000 and they need or want maximum income from this pool of capital. It is all in the bank in savings accounts earning 6 percent per year with no risk to principal. They receive $500 per month from it but they want more income.

By repositioning the entire amount to a longer term, high-yield certificate of deposit earning 8 percent, they can earn an additional $160 per month without any risk to principal. If they needed some of the principal in an emergency and had to redeem the CD early, they might lose some of their principal to redemption penalties.

By repositioning to high-yield mutual funds and stocks, they could earn 11 percent or more per year and increase the value of their principal. This would produce $400 more per month than the savings account, but their principal might fluctuate in value and they could lose part of their principal if they had to sell in an emergency and the share values were down.

The basic rule here is that the higher the yield, the higher the risk.

Use Monthly Withdrawal Programs

Many mutual funds, managed accounts, partnerships, money market accounts, and certificates can be set up to pay you on a monthly basis. Mutual funds are set up to provide for automatic monthly payments while reinvesting some income for future needs. Reinvestment of some income may enable you to offset market risks and inflation.

REDUCE INCOME TAXES

Pensions and 401K savings plans withdrawals, and many other investments, are generally fully taxable. Many retirees find themselves paying sizeable income taxes on their retirement income. There are some ways to reduce income taxes that do not reduce your income.

To reduce taxes, consider moving part of your investment capital to immediate annuities, tax-free municipal bonds, tax-free municipal bond funds, tax-free unit investment trusts, and/or purchase investments which produce low-income housing federal tax credits or historic properties tax credits.

All of these investment strategies can significantly lower income taxes or even eliminate them. The unused portion of federal tax credit programs can be carried back three years or carried forward until they are completely used. These tax credits can be used to offset annual income or lump-sum distributions from IRAs and pension programs when the employee reaches age 70½. Consult your tax professional or a financial planner to determine if the investment meets your needs and is appropriate for you.

Annuities

Immediate annuities pay monthly, quarterly, semiannually, or annually, depending on your needs. They pay guaranteed income and principal, much of which is tax free. You can stipulate the number of years you want to receive the income—the fewer the years, the higher the amount of income you will receive. Some insurance companies guarantee principal and interest. Be sure the insurance company carries an AM Best rating of A or A+.

Municipal Bonds

Some municipal bonds pay semiannual income free of federal income tax. Bonds are rated and sometimes insured. You should consider purchasing investment-grade bonds with the best yields. While tax-free income is guaranteed when bonds are insured, their value can go up or down depending on interest rates, tax law, supply and demand. When you invest amounts under $20,000, either a muncipal bond mutual fund or a unit investment trust will give you more diversity and professional management.

RETIREMENT TAX REDUCTION STRATEGIES (Continued)

Other Tax-Reduction Strategies To Consider

- Contribute to an IRA up to age 70 if you work and have salary income during retirement.
- Use charitable-giving strategies to generate tax-favored income and tax deductions during retirement.
- Own and manage rental property during retirement for tax-favored income and tax deductions.

Any tax-reduction strategies you use should be planned with the assistance and advice of your tax advisor. The largest savings for retirees may be the elimination of taxes on part of Social Security income. If individuals can reduce their income tax to $1,000 or less, they will not pay the Medicare Catastrophic Health Care surtax which is another new tax on retirees age 65 or older.

THE MEDICARE CATASTROPHIC COVERAGE ACT

On July 1, 1988, the Medicare Catastrophic Coverage Act (MCCA) was signed into law to become effective January 1, 1989. The Act brings with it the most sweeping changes to the Medicare system in 23 years.

Coverage Changes

Let us look at how the MCCA affects Part A coverages and expenses. A basic feature of the MCCA is that both current and future financing for the program and its coverages are paid for by those whom it will benefit—Medicare recipients. Most costs are borne equally by all beneficiaries, while others are paid for as utilized.

The following services have been **added** by the MCCA to already existing Medicare coverages:

- Outpatient prescription drugs
- Home intervention drug therapy
- Mammography screening
- Respite care

The following represent **increased** Part A coverages:

- Inpatient hospital coverage
- Skilled nursing facility coverage
- Home health care coverage
- Christian Science sanitorium nursing services

The following **reductions** of Part A coverages are affected:

- Inpatient hospital benefits
- Voluntary Part A premium
- Skilled nursing facility benefits
- Blood deductible

MEDICARE CATASTROPHIC COVERAGE ACT (Continued)

Premium Increases

Along with the changes in the Medicare system and its coverages, the MCCA also levies new charges on all those who are eligible for Medicare (generally those over age 65). The first such levy is the supplemental premium, which is based on an individual's or married couple's ordinary income tax liability. The second levy is an increase in the separate premium which already existed on Part B (optional) coverage.

Essentially, this amounts to new tax levies for all Medicare-eligible individuals, except that new Medicare supplemental premium payments are not required for any year where individual or joint tax liability is less than $1,000.

RECOMMENDATION

Financial planning is important now to reduce your tax bill wherever possible to under $1,000 per household to be excluded from the Medicare tax. How you structure your retirement income now becomes crucial.

Supplemental Premiums

These are paid in addition to federal income taxes. Amounts due as supplemental premium payments are calculated as follows. Individuals and married, filing jointly where both husband and wife are eligible take their *tax liability* from Form 1040 for the given year and divide it by 150. The results are then multiplied by the applicable premium rate, which is:

1989	1990	1991	1992	1993
22.50	37.50	39.00	40.50	42.00

These results are then compared to the annual ceilings which limit the required supplemental premium payments:

1989	1990	1991	1992	1993
$800	$850	$900	$950	$1050

The calculated result, up to the amount of the ceiling, is the amount each eligible individual is required to pay. If both husband and wife are eligible, then the ceiling amounts above are multiplied by two.

If married persons who do not live apart file separate returns, they are treated as both being Medicare eligible. This ensures that the supplemental premium will be paid and discourages filing separate returns unless husband and wife are indeed separated.

MEDICARE CATASTROPHIC COVERAGE ACT (Continued)

Supplemental premium payments are not treated as a tax for purposes of any deduction, tax credit, or the alternative minimum tax (federal taxes), but they are treated as a tax for purposes of estimated tax payments after 1989.

Part B Monthly Premiums

These are increased from $24.80 to $28.80 ($4 per month increase) in 1989. Increases will scale up from $4 in 1989 to $4.90 in 1990, $7.40 in 1991, $9.20 in 1992, and $10.20 in 1993. Beyond these dates, increases will be based on the cost experience of the MCCA programs.

A limit applies to these increases. If an individual's Social Security benefit increases are equal to or less than the MCCA monthly increases, then the MCCA monthly increases will be limited to the Social Security monthly benefit increase for that individual.

Ceiling on Part B Expenses

January 1, 1990, ushers in a provision which caps beneficiary co-pays under Part B. This limitation begins at $1,370 and will be inflation indexed annually. Part A expenses do not count towards this limitation, but *all* Part B co-payments and deductibles are added together to be applied to the ceiling amount.

Miscellaneous Provisions

For the *first* time ever, in response to tremendous concern raised on this issue, the MCCA includes provisions which exempt significant assets from the reaches of the Medicaid system. Persons who continue to live at home during the institutionalization of a spouse now may retain a monthly income of $786 (over two and a half times the previous $300 per month limit) and $12,000 of liquid assets (compared to $2,700 previously) without jeopardizing Medicaid eligibility of the institutionalized individual. Similar to before, the spouse may retain the home, a car, certain personal effects, and other minor items, subject to various state laws and regulations.

In another miscellaneous provision, the new law gives Medicare beneficiaries a 30-day grace period to review any Medicare supplemental coverage program purchased. If the beneficiary finds that the policy is duplicitous of the new MCCA coverages, then such beneficiary may obtain a full refund of any premiums paid if such demand is made within the 30-day grace period beginning with the purchase date of such policy.

Finally, the MCCA made no substantive changes in the area of long-term nursing home care. Medicare has never included coverage for custodial care services, which include nonskill and non-intensive care treatments and services, but there are coverages in the Medicaid program for these areas. Also, the MCCA made some changes in the areas of skilled nursing facility benefits, as mentioned above.

RECOMMENDATION

As you can see, the new MCCA provisions do not cover long-term nursing home care. In most cases, if your *company extends your health care coverage beyond retirement, it too excludes long-term nursing home coverage.* You should shop and consider purchasing your own nursing home care supplement to protect retirement income and assets. Nursing home care costs average $2,000 to $3,000 per month. This could create a severe hardship on spouse's long-term income.

CONCLUSION

Once you have built your retirement income program you can review it periodically to see that it is meeting your needs and wants. You should use a variety of advisors to review your plans from time to time to see that you are getting the best returns with safety in the marketplace. Investment circumstances and opportunities change and so must your plans. If the plan maintains your lifestyle comfortably, then it is a success.

> Remember, in retirement most people do not plan to fail, they merely fail to plan.

We have discussed many ways you can use employee benefits to build wealth and accomplish many of your financial objectives. Employee benefits, used wisely in your financial planning, can help you have the financial security and independence you want.

NOTES

NOTES

NOTES

ABOUT THE FIFTY-MINUTE SERIES

"Every so often an idea emerges that is so simple and appealing, people wonder why it didn't come along sooner. The Fifty-Minute series is just such an idea. Excellent!"

Mahaliah Levine, Vice President for Training and Development Dean Witter Reynolds, Inc.

WHAT IS A FIFTY-MINUTE BOOK?
—Fifty-Minute books are brief, soft-covered, "self-study" titles covering a wide variety of topics pertaining to business and self-improvement. They are reasonably priced, ideal for formal training, excellent for self-study and perfect for remote location training.

"A Fifty-Minute book gives the reader fundamentals that can be applied on the job, even before attending a formal class"

Lynn Baker, Manager of Training Fleming Corporation

WHY ARE FIFTY-MINUTE BOOKS UNIQUE?
—Because of their format. Designed to be "read with a pencil," the basics of a subject can be quickly grasped and applied through a series of hands-on activities, exercises and cases.

"Fifty-Minute books are the best new publishing idea in years. They are clear, practical, concise and affordable—perfect for today's world."

Leo Hauser, Past President ASTD

HOW MANY FIFTY-MINUTE BOOKS ARE THERE?
—Those listed on the following pages at this time. Additional titles are always in development. For more information write to **Crisp Publications, Inc., 95 First Street, Los Altos, CA 94022.**

THE FIFTY-MINUTE SERIES

Quantity	Title	Code #	Price	Amount
	MANAGEMENT TRAINING			
	Successful Negotiation	09-2	$7.95	
	Personal Performance Contracts	12-2	$7.95	
	Team Building	16-5	$7.95	
	Effective Meeting Skills	33-5	$7.95	
	An Honest Day's Work	39-4	$7.95	
	Managing Disagreement Constructively	41-6	$7.95	
	Training Managers To Train	43-2	$7.95	
	The Fifty-Minute Supervisor	58-0	$7.95	
	Leadership Skills For Women	62-9	$7.95	
	Systematic Problem Solving & Decision Making	63-7	$7.95	
	Coaching & Counseling	68-8	$7.95	
	Ethics in Business	69-6	$7.95	
	Understanding Organizational Change	71-8	$7.95	
	Project Management	75-0	$7.95	
	Managing Organizational Change	80-7	$7.95	
	Working Together	85-8	$7.95	
	Financial Planning With Employee Benefits	90-4	$7.95	
	PERSONNEL TRAINING & HUMAN RESOURCE MANAGEMENT			
	Effective Performance Appraisals	11-4	$7.95	
	Quality Interviewing	13-0	$7.95	
	Personal Counseling	14-9	$7.95	
	Job Performance and Chemical Dependency	27-0	$7.95	
	New Employee Orientation	46-7	$7.95	
	Professional Excellence for Secretaries	52-1	$7.95	
	Guide To Affirmative Action	54-8	$7.95	
	Writing A Human Resource Manual	70-X	$7.95	
	COMMUNICATIONS			
	Effective Presentation Skills	24-6	$7.95	
	Better Business Writing	25-4	$7.95	
	The Business of Listening	34-3	$7.95	
	Writing Fitness	35-1	$7.95	
	The Art of Communicating	45-9	$7.95	
	Technical Presentation Skills	55-6	$7.95	
	Making Humor Work	61-0	$7.95	
	Visual Aids in Business	77-7	$7.95	
	Speedreading in Business	78-5	$7.95	
	Influencing Others: A Practical Guide	84-X	$7.95	
	SELF-MANAGEMENT			
	Balancing Home And Career	10-6	$7.95	
	Mental Fitness: A Guide to Emotional Health	15-7	$7.95	
	Personal Financial Fitness	20-3	$7.95	
	Attitude: Your Most Priceless Possession	21-1	$7.95	
	Personal Time Management	22-X	$7.95	

(Continued on next page)

THE FIFTY-MINUTE SERIES

Quantity	Title	Code #	Price	Amount
	SELF-MANAGEMENT (CONTINUED)			
	Preventing Job Burnout	23-8	$7.95	
	Successful Self-Management	26-2	$7.95	
	Developing Positive Assertiveness	38-6	$7.95	
	Time Management And The Telephone	53-X	$7.95	
	Memory Skills In Business	56-4	$7.95	
	Developing Self-Esteem	66-1	$7.95	
	Creativity In Business	67-X	$7.95	
	Managing Personal Change	74-2	$7.95	
	Winning At Human Relations	86-6	$7.95	
	Stop Procrastinating	88-2	$7.95	
	SALES TRAINING/QUALITY CUSTOMER SERVICE			
	Sales Training Basics	02-5	$7.95	
	Restaurant Server's Guide	08-4	$7.95	
	Quality Customer Service	17-3	$7.95	
	Telephone Courtesy And Customer Service	18-1	$7.95	
	Professional Selling	42-4	$7.95	
	Customer Satisfaction	57-2	$7.95	
	Telemarketing Basics	60-2	$7.95	
	Calming Upset Customers	65-3	$7.95	
	Quality At Work	72-6	$7.95	
	Managing A Quality Service Organization	83-1	$7.95	
	ENTREPRENEURSHIP			
	Marketing Your Consulting Or Professional Services	40-8	$7.95	
	Starting Your Small Business	44-0	$7.95	
	Publicity Power	82-3	$7.95	
	CAREER GUIDANCE & STUDY SKILLS			
	Study Skills Strategies	05-X	$7.95	
	Career Discovery	07-6	$7.95	
	Plan B: Protecting Your Career From The Winds of Change	48-3	$7.95	
	I Got The Job!	59-9	$7.95	
	OTHER CRISP INC. BOOKS			
	Comfort Zones: A Practical Guide For Retirement Planning	00-9	$13.95	
	Stepping Up To Supervisor	11-8	$13.95	
	The Unfinished Business Of Living: Helping Aging Parents	19-X	$12.95	
	Managing Performance	23-7	$18.95	
	Be True To Your Future: A Guide to Life Planning	47-5	$13.95	
	Up Your Productivity	49-1	$10.95	
	How To Succeed In A Man's World	79-3	$7.95	
	Practical Time Management	275-4	$13.95	
	Copyediting: A Practical Guide	51-3	$18.95	

THE FIFTY-MINUTE SERIES
(Continued)

☐ Send volume discount information.

☐ Please send me a catalog.

	Amount
Total (from other side)	
Shipping ($1.50 first book, $.50 per title thereafter)	
California Residents add 7% tax	
Total	

Ship to: ______________________

____

____

____

Phone number: ______________________

Bill to: ______________________

____

____

____

P.O. # ______________________

All orders except those with a P.O.# must be prepaid.
For more information Call (415) 949-4888 or FAX (415) 949-1610.

NO POSTAGE
NECESSARY
IF MAILED
IN THE
UNITED STATES

BUSINESS REPLY
FIRST CLASS PERMIT NO. 884 LOS ALTOS, CA

POSTAGE WILL BE PAID BY ADDRESSEE

Crisp Publications, Inc.
95 First Street
Los Altos, CA 94022